Endorsements

First There is an awe-inspiring journey through the life, formation, and impact of Medal of Honor recipient—Air Force Master Sergeant John Chapman. From his growing up in "Norman Rockwellian" Connecticut, through his high-intensity special tactics career to his final heroic fight in the mountains of Afghanistan, *First There* reveals how faith, family, friends, and trials forged this homegrown boy into an elite special operations Combat Controller. With wit, candor, insight, and love, Lori relates a captivating story of the making of an American hero—one who would save the lives of scores of his brother warriors in Afghanistan at the cost of his own.

Colonel Ken Rodriguez, USAF (Retired)

A wonderful book. Lori offers readers profound insights into the life of one of the USAF's greatest heroes, John Chapman. While many first encountered Chapman through *Alone at Dawn*, this new work dives deeper into his personal journey. Lori's exceptional storytelling talent crafts an intimate portrait of John's life, revealing the foundational influences from his family that shaped him into a prominent figure in USAF history. Even as someone who knew John as a friend and teammate, I have now gained a richer understanding of the experiences that defined him and contributed to his legacy.

CMSgt Mike West, USAF (retired)

i

The last time I saw Chappy was when we exchanged apartment keys in Virginia Beach, as we came to replace them on alert, and they were heading to Afghanistan to replace the original surge after the 9/11 attacks. As always, he was calm, cool, and collected—ever-ready to perform his duty. That was my last handshake with him. The news came later that a teammate had perished in Takur Ghar, crushing the morale of the team. When we heard it was John, it hurt even more.

Very few humans are fortunate to be in the company of warriors like John Chapman. For those of us who served alongside him, we got to see an unchained spirit fueled by courage, loyalty, and dedication. From home to the battlefield, Chappy was consistently committed to being the best. How does a man become the type of example that Chappy was? We have to understand his upbringing, his team dynamics in his profession, and his family life.

In this book, Lori does a magnificent job in walking us through a timeline of memories that helps the reader understand Chappy at a granular level. From childhood memories to his early teenage years to his journey to becoming a Combat Controller, this book serves as a precursor of a famed story of valor and courage. Preceding the days of Robert's Ridge, we get to see Chappy through many different lenses, adding context to why he did what he did on that fateful day. It was just who he was, and he performed to the best of his abilities until he could do no more.

Sit back and enjoy the story of a man with high morals, extreme courage, and love for humankind.

Chappy, you are forever missed, but how fortunate are we to have your family, our team, and scores of others that continue to keep your memory alive. First There, That Others May Live . . .

Ramon "CZ" Colon-Lopez, SEAC (Ret.)

FIRST THERE

The Life and Legacy of
American Hero MSgt John Chapman

LORI CHAPMAN LONGFRITZ

First There: The Life and Legacy of American Hero MSgt John Chapman

Copyright © 2025 by Lori Chapman Longfritz

Publisher Information
Lori Chapman Longfritz
Cheyenne, WY 82009

For more information or to contact the author, please email theloloproject24@gmail.com

ISBN 979-8-9920542-0-0 (hardcover)
ISBN 979-8-9920542-2-4 (softcover)
ISBN 979-8-9920542-1-7 (eBook)

Cover design: Terry Dugan
Cover photo credit:
        Flag–AlenKadr@Adobe Stock
        Background–pe3check@Adobe Stock
Editorial team: Marcus Costantino, Josh Vogt, Cristina Wright, and Amy Sinnott
Interior design: eBookBurner Technologies
Publishing services provided by BelieversBookServices.com

First printing: 2025
Printed in the United States of America

Dedicated to:

My mom Terry, who raised four pretty damn good kids,
if I do say so myself; my brother Kevin, who never
failed to keep life interesting; and to my sister Tammy,
with whom I share silly sisterly fun and secret codes.
I love you all.

Contents

Commendation

In the early aftermath of the death of Combat Controller and American Hero John Chapman, I came into regular contact with his extraordinary family. It was there that I first met John's fiery, vivacious and utterly unique sister Lori Chapman. I immediately took a liking to this straight-talking and down to earth gal, a liking that developed into respect and eventually a life-long friendship. At the time, I was John's squadron commander, and he and I were both members of the elite special operations counter-terrorist unit—the 24th Special Tactic Squadron based out of Ft. Bragg/Pope Air Force Base North Carolina. (now Pope Army Airfield.)

To be honest, I expected Lori, and for that matter the rest of John's family, not to have much "love" for the commanding officer who had sent her brother off on what was to be his final and fatal mission. The opposite was true, as Lori, and all of John's family, welcomed me and all of John's teammates into their homes and into their hearts.

Lori's first book, *Alone at Dawn*, co-authored with my friend and teammate Dano Schilling, focused primarily on John's courageous actions and those of his fellow special operators during Operation ANACONDA in Afghanistan in 2002, and the desperate battle atop Takur Ghar Mountain for which John was posthumously awarded the Medal of Honor. Woven into the account is a concise history of Air Force Combat Controllers—but due to the book's scope, we get only a brief glimpse into John's life, formation, and training.

Enter now, *First There*, the fulfillment of Lori's two-decade long dream of bringing her brother's full story to life. This is a mesmerizing deep-dive into the making of an American hero—from his earliest childhood years up to his last fateful day of deadly close combat in the snowy heights of the Hindu Kush mountains. From a precocious youngster, through spirited teen years, young adulthood, to his development into a superlative special operator, Lori takes us on a captivating tour of the formation of a man of faith, competence, commitment, and courage.

This is a fascinating full portrait of a man who was both consummate prankster and altruistic champion of the little guy; the hometown Joe who would fax copies of his bare ass to unsuspecting victims but also stand up to the class bully (and knock him down with a roundhouse kick). And Lori does not hold back. We get the good, the bad, and the ugly: where her brother soared and where he crash-landed. (Including some "shit" stories a less courageous author would never attempt.)

Lori's enthralling epic ranges from Capra-esque accounts of growing up in small-town America to the challenges of making it through one of the military's most grueling special operator training programs. She wonderfully recounts the ups, downs, successes, and failures, as well as the succession of people that contributed to the forging of the hero of Takur Ghar. She includes numerous "other voices" in her work to include family members, hometown buddies, fellow warriors . . . and even some souls who come out of the woodwork to attest to John's impact on their lives. In one of the many prophetic passages of the book, John remarks to sister Tammy as he was deploying to Afghanistan: "I will do anything in my power to protect my team." Lori observes: "He was a man of his word to the end."

First There simultaneously tells three love stories. First, John and the love of his birth family; next, John's love for his wife Valerie and daughters Madison and Brianna; and lastly, his love for his brothers-in-arms—consummated in the giving of his life for his team and eighteen other warriors who, due to John's actions, would live to fight another day.

If you've ever wondered what goes into the making of a hero, whether he is born or made, or if you've ever asked the question "what compels a man to give up everything; his very life for the sake of another?" Lori wonders these things too. She finds answers in the pages of *First There*. In taking this journey with her, we find these answers as well.

Colonel Ken Rodriguez, USAF (Retired)

Foreword

In a quiet corner of her living room, John Chapman's mother keeps a tiny oil lamp—a trinket brought home from a kindergarten field trip. It's a humble thing, with red and blue swirls softened by time. Yet it reveals so much about the little boy who thought first of his mom, even then. Like so many objects left behind by those we love, it's both ordinary and sacred.

John's name invokes a snowy Afghan ridge—alone at dawn, captured on video for the world to see. Yet that final stand wasn't everything he was, only the pinnacle of a life driven by love and purpose. I never served alongside John or heard his trademark laugh. Still, he feels present in my life. Maybe it's the black-and-white photo that greets me every day at work: John, dusty and battle-weary, cradling a wide-eyed Afghan child, floral pattern on the wall. In that moment, I see the caring spirit that once brought an oil lamp home to his mom—a quiet promise that human compassion can shine even in the harshest places. I see it again in the way John's family pours themselves into the causes that bear his name. And the raw footage of his final hours lingers in my mind, with a drone's unblinking eye revealing a man whose human light cut through the coldness of war.

When the Chapman family came into my life, it was already a decade removed from John's last stand.

However, as fate would have it, my two kids were the same age as his when they lost their father. So, as I wrestled with the many challenges and aspirations of being a new dad, his sacrifice felt especially poignant. I often wonder how he found the strength in those final moments, knowing all he was leaving behind. In raising my kids, I try to honor his gift by talking about heroism, service, and what it means to stand for something bigger than ourselves. Still, I always find my efforts wanting.

Now, his sister Lori invites us beyond that mountaintop and into the everyday stories behind the heroism. Through her words, we glimpse John not only in those last hours but as a kindhearted son, brother, husband, and father. We discover the mischievous boy who once hoisted a friend's bike high into a tree for a laugh—then climbed back up in remorse to retrieve it; the Combat Controller who forged unbreakable bonds with teammates; and the devoted father who whispered promises to his little girls. And, in seeing him whole, we learn how his momentous final stand came to be—not from inevitability, but from choice.

Those choices found their ultimate test in March 2002, during the early stages of the war on terror, when John's elite special operations unit attempted to rescue a fallen teammate atop an Afghan mountain stronghold. On that day, the future met the past—drones circled the skies while soldiers on horseback crossed timeworn trails. Outnumbered and under fire, John charged into an enemy-occupied bunker, freeing his teammates to move toward cover. Even after taking multiple gunshot wounds, he kept fighting. If you haven't seen the overhead drone footage of that day, I urge you to seek it out. It stands among the most staggering and inspiring displays of human courage I've ever encountered.

And still, his actions extended well beyond Takur Ghar's peak. It altered his family's path, forcing them to balance grief with keeping his spirit alive. It molded his teammates, who carry the weight of his courage. And it stirred a nation, which seldom witnesses the true costs borne by the few for the freedom of the many. In the aftermath, we remember real sacrifice is never contained in a single moment. It reverberates across the years in the lives of those left behind.

Lori's words gently lead us through those echoes. She shows us that grief and sacrifice aren't endings; they're invitations to live more fully. Perhaps we're not called to stand on a snow-capped peak and stare down a machine gun nest, but in the everyday demands of life, heroism can be found in the choices we make and the kindness we extend. Like John, we can see the highest stakes, feel the deepest fear, and remain standing anyway.

In that tiny lamp—now a family keepsake—I see the continuity between John the boy and John the man. A modest relic of childhood generosity has become a priceless symbol of his eternal courage. Let it guide us, just as John once guided others. Lori's heartfelt account proves heroism often takes root in simple love, steady loyalty, and the silent resolve to do what must be done.

I hope these pages bring you closer to John Chapman. I hope they remind you that a life isn't measured by the years we have, but by the choices we make—both in the small moments that shape our days and at those decisive turning points when everything is on the line.

Colonel Mike Wendelken is a United States Air Force Special Tactics Officer, which gives him the privilege of working for the "John Chapmans" of today's generation. Presently, he commands the 724th Special Tactics Group, which continues the proud lineage of John's final assignment. The views expressed here are his alone and do not necessarily reflect the positions of the United States Air Force or the 724th Special Tactics Group.

Preface

My brother was Air Force Combat Controller (CCT), Technical Sergeant John "Chappy" Chapman, posthumously promoted to Master Sergeant on August 24, 2018. John's career field is part of our military's special tactics (ST) world. It's dangerous. It's physically, mentally, and emotionally taxing. It's not for the faint of heart, and only the very best of the best succeed in becoming a Controller. Their motto is "First There" because—they are.

John was embedded with a SEAL team when he was left alone to endure a fierce, hour's long firefight on top of Takur Ghar mountain in Afghanistan on March 4, 2002. John risked death to protect his team and then sacrificed his life for eighteen others—all but one he had never met.

From the moment I got "the call" that we had lost my brother, I've wanted to share the story of his life. It has taken over two decades to write the book I envisioned. My first book *Alone at Dawn* tells the story of Combat Control, shares tiny glimpses of John's life and his journey to become a Controller, and tells the ugly truth of the battle during which he was killed. I am extremely proud of the book because it is *the* source for facts about what happened that early March morning—information that slowly came to light days, months, and even years later. It has been dubbed by some as the chronicle of his life, but it isn't. It's powerful, yes—an absolute must-read. But it doesn't chronicle John's life; it tells of his bravery at the *end* of it. I had to fulfill my dream of honoring him, so this book is John's story, enmeshed with mine and those of so many others, told through my memories and stories from people to whom I am eternally grateful.

I want to introduce John to those who never knew him and share stories that his friends and family may not have heard. I want the reader to laugh and be moved by John's life as much as I was in sharing it, and I've written it in a way no one else could. It would not have been possible without the help of countless family and friends who knew and loved him. My first and best source was our mom Terry and, honestly, she helped me accomplish something that I did primarily for her. She is so proud of all four of us, but Kevin, Tammy, and I still are adding to our stories. John's story has ended, and I want to ensure it's not forgotten. I cannot thank Mom enough for searching her heart for precious memories that show John for the character he was and the integrity he had.

Others of my family also shared memories, and John's story could never be complete without them. I appreciate their willingness to let us peek into their time with him—to share sometimes painful recollections so you may know John as they did. Stories from John's widow show him from his most helpless to some of his goofiest moments. I am equally grateful that our dad wrote a letter to the commander of John's last unit, the 24th Special Tactics Squadron (A.K.A. "the two four"). Dad passed away two years after John so, without his letter, we would have lost John's thought process through some important events.

John's childhood friends graciously shared memories, and I think talking about him so many years later was cathartic. Laughter replaced the tears that would have come years before, and that is exactly how John would want it to be. Thank you to John's best friends with whom he shared countless adventures, some of which we may never know, and whose friendships he never let slip away. Thanks also to those who were in John's life for a short time but were willing to share how he affected them. And I am grateful to the complete stranger who reached out with the sweet and unique way she chose to honor John. Readers will love her story!

I offer my heartfelt thanks to John's military brothers who fought through foggy memories to share some very cool stories about him from their training days and CCT years—stories that would be lost to the warrior winds had they not dug deep. They helped me complete the picture of who John was at his core. Some of you were only in John's life briefly, and some for much longer, but this book would not be whole without all of your input. I am eternally grateful for your help in telling his story.

Finally, thank you, dear reader, for wanting to know more about John and for joining me on this journey to share him with you. He was a unique character, but my desire is that you see a little, or a lot, of yourself in him, in our small-town upbringing, or in something he did. And, if nothing else, I hope you are greatly entertained by his antics.

Prologue

When duty calls, that is when character counts.
~ William Safire

Like a giant rock dropped into the middle of a lake, the events of September 11, 2001, rippled outward from the World Trade Center in New York City, the Pentagon in Washington, DC, and a quiet field in Somerset, Pennsylvania. They sent palpable waves over geographical space and time—time now measured in decades.

Like most Americans of a certain age, I will never forget where I was on that awful morning. The evil actions of the day didn't directly affect my life right then, but they soon changed it forever. My day started at 8:00 a.m. in the Small Claims Office at Manchester Superior Court in Manchester, Connecticut. A radio sounded softly from the corner behind my desk. Shortly after 8:45, the DJ announced that a small plane had hit one of the World Trade Center towers in New York City, 130 miles away. We were concerned but not alarmed because it felt so far removed from us.

Twenty minutes later, the DJ interrupted again with a disturbing update, his voice wavering; it was *not* a small airplane but a passenger aircraft that had hit the North Tower, and a second aircraft had just plowed into the South Tower. No one knew what to think as the gravity of what happened was sinking in. The tiny employee lounge had the only television in the building, so I headed there to find it already crammed with anxious people. As we watched in horror, my immediate thought was of my brother John. I leaned hard against the wall, feeling as though I might collapse, and said aloud, "My brother is going. Oh my God, he has to go."

But to where?

I rushed back to my desk to call John, not knowing what to say or if I'd even reach him. He answered immediately. How long we talked was a blur, but he confirmed he would be going "somewhere." He said he would do what he had trained to do, and he would go wherever he was told to go. He stopped mid-sentence then yelled, "Holy shit! The top of one of the towers is falling. I have to go." We said our hurried goodbyes and I love yous and hung up.

I felt sick—physically ill. Looking around, I saw the shock on the faces of those around me. The courthouse closed due to its proximity to NYC and the uncertainty of other attacks. Once home, I turned on the television to discover that the Pentagon had also been hit and another flight had vanished. Like millions, I was glued to the screen, watching, crying, cursing, and praying. I hugged my daughter tightly and watched the coverage as it played over and over again.

In the weeks after that hateful day, many of us contacted John to find out when he'd be leaving America for…somewhere. At point, everything was so fluid, I'm sure even those in charge didn't have an exact plan yet, but John sent a group email on September 23, 2001, with the subject line: "Still here." The body of his email was short and to the point:

> Hello from NC, To all the family and friends that have me in their thoughts and prayers. I am still here in Fayetteville. A few diplomatic efforts have to be accomplished before Uncle Sam can deploy to someone else's soil. I have appreciated all of the phone calls and words of encouragement. This is going to be a sustained effort by the US to rid the world of some truly evil people. I just hope everyone is ready to get there (sic) hands dirty. Heaven knows we already have them bloody. Love from NC, John.

I remember reading it for the first time and feeling a sense of foreboding and fear—for the future and our country but mostly for John.

I consider September 11, 2001, to be the day John's death was set into motion. Six months later, he deployed on his final mission to a desolate mountaintop in Afghanistan. It was poorly planned by incompetent "leaders" and was unnecessary, and John paid for that hubris with his life.

By now, the world knows the truth of what happened on that mission. They know the extent of his heroism—that he risked his life for one fallen teammate and other members of his team, and then gave his life for eighteen others, mostly strangers, who comprised the

Quick Reaction Force called in to save his remaining five teammates. On August 22, 2018, President Donald Trump posthumously awarded John the Medal of Honor in recognition of his actions on March 4, 2002.

Search John's name on the Internet and countless links will appear that describe what he did to save his team on Takur Ghar. Most of those accounts are not completely factual. *Alone at Dawn* fills the gaps of what the Internet articles fail to expose and accurately records his heroic actions and death. What will not be found on those Internet pages, or even in most of my book, is who he was at his core that enabled him to do what he did in his last hours. And that is why, though this book does include portions of his end-of-life story, it is not about the battle. It's about his "dash"—the time between birth and death.

When John was in second grade, he ran all the way home from school and burst through the back door, out of breath, grinning from ear to ear, and waving a book over his head like a wild man. The book was *Johnny Appleseed.* He got it from school; it must have been a Scholastic Books order, and he was delirious about it, "Johnny Appleseed has *my* name! My name is in a book!" In my very short life experience, I had never known someone whose name was in a book, so I was impressed and, let's be honest, probably a little jealous. For some time after that day, Mom called him Johnny Appleseed, and at Christmas that year, he gave Mom and Dad a handmade card signed, "Love, Johnny Appleseed."

I have thought about those thirty seconds of our lives many times over the years and the irony of the story is glaring. Decades later, John not only has his name in many books, magazines, and newspaper and Internet articles, but he is in *history* books—the records of our nation. His uncontrollable excitement of yesteryear would be greatly tempered with humility if he could see his name in books now, but I must put him in at least one more. Unlike all those other books, this one is about his *life*—the boy I grew up with; the boy who affected countless lives over the course of his; the boy who lived with honor and integrity and who grew into the man who sacrificed his life for teammates and country. It is about a man who lived the way he died—on *his* terms and a hero to so many.

As John's integrity, compassion, and moral compass unfold, readers will begin to understand why I chose *First There* for my title. He was not only first there while a CCT, but he was also first there in countless ways for so many people throughout his life.

PART ONE

The Early Years and Young Adulthood

*The key to immortality is first living
a life worth remembering.*
~ Bruce Lee

1

Chapman Family—
How It All Began

Children will not remember you for the
material things you provided but for the
feeling that you cherished them.
~ Richard L. Evans

Is it possible to tell from the moment a baby is born that
he or she is destined for greatness? Can we know in an
instant that the baby will be a hero? The short answer is,
"Of course not." But at the *end* of a hero's life, the age-
old question arises: Was it nature or nurture that shaped
this person?

Following John's life story, each passing day, each
passing month, each passing year, one finds clues that
eventually lead, like a trail of breadcrumbs, to the
realization that he was great—a hero on many levels and
at various times in his life. If you trace those breadcrumbs
back through time, some of them so tiny you would
almost miss them, the clues become more obvious
than when they were happening. In connecting the dots

backward, they reveal "ah-ha!" moments in which the observer can say, "Wow! That really shows the type of person he was," or "*That's* why he did what he did."

Then begs the next questions: Do those breadcrumbs indicate he came by greatness naturally? Would he have turned out so wonderfully no matter his upbringing? Did the nurturing he received throughout his life form those heroic moments? Or is it as I believe, a combination of nature *and* nurture, the ratio of which is impossible to measure?

When I decided to share John's life, I debated where to start. On the surface, he was an ordinary kid with an unremarkable small-town upbringing. Upon further consideration, though, he was an extraordinary human being from the time he could barely talk. I had my answer: Start from the beginning.

Mom had always dreamed of having four children, and in her fantasy, they would be boy, girl, boy, girl. Well, there are four of us kids—Kevin, Lori, John, and Tammy—and we're so close in age (Mom had us all within five years) that I don't remember a time that it *wasn't* the four of us. If Mom had told me we were quadruplets, I might have believed her. Together, we laughed and cried, played and fought, got into trouble, and usually had a lot of fun. As with all typical sibling love/hate relationships, we could be fighting amongst ourselves one second and defending each other the next.

Kevin is the oldest. He is usually pretty quiet, which belies how very smart and curious he is. One night when he was three years old, Mom and Dad took him and me (an infant) to the Eastfield Mall in Eastfield,

Massachusetts. We had just moved from Michigan, and it was our first time going to the mall. In a moment of distraction, Kevin got separated from us, leaving Mom and Dad to frantically search for him, calling his name and checking possible hiding spots. They were getting desperate, and Dad finally said, "Let's go look in the parking lot." When they approached the car, Kevin was leaning against it with his arms crossed and he asked, "What took you so long?" He was *three*—in a place he had never been and at night!

Sometimes, his intelligence backfired on him. In fourth grade, Kevin got himself in trouble by refusing to do his vocabulary homework. When Mom asked him why, he shrugged and said, "I already know it; why should I have to do it again at home?" That attitude did not fly with his teacher and, much to his dislike, he still had to complete the work. Kevin brought some interesting times to our childhood and, although we're all smart, he might have been a little smarter—a deep thinker.

I am the next in line—the rebel, I suppose. I believed girls could do almost anything a boy could, and I set out to prove my theory. We all had chores to do, and I railed against doing "girly" work like washing the dishes and doing the laundry, especially for all six of us. Mom and Dad were constantly questioned, "Why can't the boys do the laundry, and Tammy and I can do stuff outside?" I'm not sure Tammy was on board with my argument, but I dragged her into it anyway. I was also the mouthy one, which should come as no surprise to those who know me. I was opinionated and not afraid to speak up, but I was also very independent and stubborn from an early age.

When I was eighteen months old, our neighbors had two swing sets next to each other. I climbed the smaller one to get onto the larger set, sat on the crossbar, and flipped upside down. Mom saw me from the kitchen window just as I flung myself backward, and she tore out of the house terrified that I would fall and break my neck. She pulled me down, smacked my butt, and sternly told me not to go up there again. By the time she got back into the kitchen, I was up on the tall crossbar, swinging upside down. Mom shook her head as she realized, "This child is going to test me."

At eight years old, I started playing soccer for the town league but there were no girls' teams. It took a couple of years before the town had them, and when I got to high school, there was still no girls' team. At the end of my freshman year, five of us marched into the principal's office and told him, "If we don't have a girls' team next year, we're all trying out for the boys' team." We had a team the very next year. I don't know about the rest of them, but I most certainly would have shown up at the boys' tryouts.

John shared the middle child slot with me. He claimed the position of family jokester, making good times even better and tough times seem not quite so bad. John lived carefree, adventurous, and, in some ways, ahead of his time when he interacted with others. Long before kids were taught that no one should be bullied or left out, he befriended outcasts because he knew it was right, and he didn't care who saw them together. He defended those who couldn't defend themselves. Don't get me wrong, John could also be quite mischievous—something you'll discover throughout this book.

Tammy rounded out the Chapman four. Another quiet observer like Kevin, she watched what didn't work for the rest of us and made mental notes not to repeat our mistakes. Tammy also fiercely defended her family.

One night, the four of us were out front playing a game of tag. Kevin was a sophomore at that point, John and I were in middle school, and Tammy was a fifth grader. As we ran around, a group of older high schoolers— three boys and two girls—walked by our yard. They got mouthy with us, and we got "brave" back at them. Eventually, our tit-for-tat wasn't enough. They told us to meet them at the elementary school for an ass-whooping. When we said we weren't going to show up, they came inside the hedges, and one of the girls challenged me to a fight. We ended up grappling on the ground, and, at one point, the girl's rear end stuck out from our ball of intertwined arms and legs. Tammy didn't hesitate; she stepped close, pulled her foot back, and landed it hard on the girl's butt.

I would *not* want to be on the receiving end of her kick; she had a powerful strike. Tammy's contribution pretty much ended the fight, and the kids went on their way, shouting threats as they did. We laughed about Tammy literally "kicking her ass" and it took some time for the adrenalin to subside. Her role as defender has never changed—Don't mess with Mama Bear. But as tough as she could be in defense of her family, Tammy also drew little ones to her. They felt her kind heart and gravitated toward her—the little pied piper. They still do.

As a group, we were a force to be reckoned with—all for one and one for all. And though this book is about John, it's worth mentioning that I loved growing up with Kevin and Tammy too. They are special people. I am blessed that they're my family, and they are so much more dynamic than just "the quiet ones."

Our parents were a good team back then too. As the breadwinner, Dad worked for United Airlines at Bradley International Airport in our hometown. He made sure we understood that Mom came first; he never tolerated any disrespect toward her. He also sacrificed sleep, averaging about three hours a night, to coach several soccer teams when we were in our teens. As disciplinarian, Dad came up with unique punishments throughout the years, and as mentor, he found novel ways of teaching us life lessons. Some of those punitions and counsel are shared here.

Mom stayed home in our early years, encouraging us to try new things, making sure we did our best in school, and loving us no matter what. She was our biggest fan in all we did and was either directly involved or in the front row cheering us on. Mom chauffeured us to all events. Can you imagine having to cart around FOUR kids, sometimes in two or three directions? She was our nurse for physical pain and broken hearts. She was our chef, or should I say "cook" because the cuisine was very basic. With six mouths to feed and one income, we had lots of spaghetti and hamburger meals. One of my favorites was when she made breakfast for dinner, a concept that flipped the script back then. Now, it's no big deal, but having scrambled eggs with ham and potatoes was a special treat back in the day. Mom was June Cleaver, minus the high heels and pearls.

Let me back up to where it all started: Teresa Kennedy, Terry to those who want her to respond, was born and raised in Hamilton Township just outside of Trenton, New Jersey. At age eighteen, she and her girlfriends enjoyed dancing at the local USO in Trenton, which also attracted young airmen from nearby McGuire AFB and soldiers from Fort Dix. Eugene "Gene" Chapman was stationed at McGuire and went to the USO dances frequently to "meet the ladies." He met Mom at one of those dances, and the rest, as they always seem to say, is history.

They married in 1961 and moved to Michigan where Dad grew up. He had worked for Capital Airlines in high school, which by then had merged with United Airlines, and he returned to it after his short stint in the Air Force. Dad worked at the local airport while Mom stayed home, first with Kevin, and then with me too. By the time she was pregnant with John, she and Dad desperately wanted to leave Michigan. They settled in Enfield, Connecticut, a small town ten minutes away from Dad's new job at the airport in Windsor Locks, also home to the "Flying Yankees," the Connecticut Air National Guard 103rd Airlift Wing.

Dad settled in at Bradley, and Mom prepared for baby number three. She should have known from the moment she went into labor that there would never be a dull moment with John. He was past his due date, and the doctors were going to induce labor if he didn't come on his own. One hot and humid July night in 1965, she and Dad went to the stock car races at Agawam Speedway in Agawam, Massachusetts. Walking to the car afterward, Mom grabbed Dad's arm and said, "We need to go to the hospital. I think I'm going to have the baby." Kevin and I had already been shipped off to Grandma and Grandpa's house in New Jersey a few weeks prior, so their only concern was getting to the hospital in nearby Springfield, Massachusetts. It was fifteen minutes away, and Dad made it there in ten, leaving Mom with the maternity nurses while he parked the car.

Fathers didn't usually go into delivery rooms in 1965, so, while Dad took up residence in the waiting room, Mom labored alone in the birthing room packed with a group of doctors and nurses. While a modest woman, childbirth left no room for modesty. An epidural had numbed her from the waist down, but nothing could numb her mind as she listened to the doctors speaking to nurses as though she weren't even in the room. "He's too big for her; should have had a c-section." But it was too late for that; he was already in the birth canal. She thought she heard, "He's breech," as she felt her body being pushed and tugged. Mom's heart raced with concern for her unborn baby. She developed a quick onset of toxemia during delivery, and the nurses began moving with urgency. Toxemia causes the mother's blood pressure to rise sharply and swelling of the face, hands, and feet develops, creating an extremely dangerous situation for mother and baby. The only cure for toxemia is birth. Mom *had* to deliver her baby boy, and fast!

On Wednesday, July 14, 1965, at 6:13 a.m., John Allan Chapman finally made his presence known with a shaky, primal cry that only newly born babies make. He was nine pounds, one ounce, and twenty-three inches long, with blue eyes and barely-there light brown hair on his adorably giant head. John had been a month late, only making his entrance into the world when he was good and ready, and it was on his terms—a maxim he held throughout his life.

Because of John's birth weight and dramatic delivery, Mom's doctor told her not to get pregnant for at least two years; the turning and tugging had messed her up pretty well. She held off on her dream of having four kids as long as she could.

In 1966, we moved from Enfield to Windsor Locks where Mom and Dad bought a light green, three-bedroom, ranch-style house on a corner lot on Andover Road. It had a small kitchen, a good-sized living room, and one tiny bathroom packed into 1,000 square feet. The basement was mostly unfinished but, somehow, we made it work. Hedges bordered the yard, and the cracked driveway started on Andover Road, curved around the back of the house, and ended on Cornwall Drive. The house was built in the 1950s as military housing and was a mile from Dad's job at Bradley Airport. It was situated directly under the approach for one of the runways. Airplanes descending for landing were so low as they passed over our house that we could wave to people in the window seats and watch them wave back. The aircraft were a source of entertainment, wonder, and security for us over the years. As long as we could feel the *thump, thump* in our chests from the blade slaps of Air National Guard helicopters, and as long as passenger jets screeched overhead with certain regularity in their graceful descents, we had a sense that all was right in our world.

In July 1967, a year after moving, Tammy became the fourth little Chapman. She was born well within the time deemed safe by the doctor, but Mom had no difficulties, and Tammy was perfect. Mom had her four children—boy, girl, boy, girl.

2

Windsor Locks, Connecticut

There are things about growing up in a small town that
you can't necessarily quantify.
~ Brandon Routh

The opening quote for this chapter perfectly describes
how I feel about our little town: Mr. Routh is not wrong,
but I will try my best to do just that—quantify it.

Windsor Locks and its people were an important part
of our upbringing. Collectively, they were like another
family member helping shape who we were then and
affecting who we are now. It is steeped in history dating
back to the late 1820s. The Connecticut River runs along
the town's eastern border, and Windsor Locks became an
important stop for river travelers. Waterfalls five miles
north of town forced the creation of the Windsor Locks
Canal in 1829 so people could navigate around them.
The town took its name from the canal locks used to
move boats up and down the river. Though the locks have
been inoperable since the 1970s, locals and visitors hike
and cycle along the canal towpath beside the beautifully
scenic river.

Officially, Windsor Locks covers about nine square miles, but the reality is that Bradley Airport and the Air National Guard occupy one-third of it. Both are bordered by Route 75, which is known as Ella Grasso Turnpike, named for a "townie" and the first US woman to be elected governor.

The town was built on the rich soil of the Tobacco Valley, named for the shade tobacco once grown in the region, which is why everything from trees and bushes to animals and birds flourish there. Mature hardwood trees—elm, oak, and maple—thrive along its narrow streets, offering shade on hot summer days, and creating canopies bursting with the colors of fire when the cold days of fall arrive. As winter approaches, the browned leaves drop from their branches and float aimlessly to the ground, creating a crunchy ground cover that no one can resist *swishing* through. We spent many autumn weekends raking leaves into huge piles and then rolling around in them until crushed leaves stuck to our clothing and buried in our hair. The leaves smelled of musty wood, a clear indicator that fall was almost over.

Winter usually turned Windsor Locks into a giant snow globe, as the falling leaves of autumn morphed into glistening snowflakes that clung to the first thing they touched. The snow brought anticipation of days off from school and the collection of Wonder Bread® bags. With every wet snowfall, we were giddy, hoping school would be canceled so we could shove our feet into bag-lined boots and meet friends for snowball fights, snowmen, and snow forts. Sometimes we trudged to Denslow Park for an afternoon of ice skating, while other times we headed to the Windsor Locks Middle School to sled down the long, steep hill behind it. Wonder Bread® bags aside, winters in Windsor Locks are the same today, and, no matter the activity, New England winters bring wet, heavy snow that is perfect for all of it.

Once in a great while, freezing rain turned the town into a shimmering ice sculpture as it did in 1973 when the power went out for several days. We were more fortunate than some; we had a gas stove and could cook hot meals, but the house was unbearably cold. Decades later, when my husband was renovating the house for Mom, he discovered the exterior walls were only two-and-a-half inches thick and had minimal insulation. It's no wonder we had to huddle together in the living room during that power outage, fully dressed in our winter jackets and long johns!

Not to be outdone by Jack Frost, spring was gloriously green as the elms and oaks awakened from their winter nap, and the buds on flowering shrubs opened like a beautifully orchestrated ballet. Striking colors blanketed the town, from the pale pink of Mountain Laurels to the bright yellow of Marigolds, and the flaming leaves of red maple trees. The blossoming plants attracted an equally colorful array of birds—bluejays, American goldfinches, and cardinals—and the sound of their songs signaled that spring had officially arrived. Gray squirrels raced from yard to yard and tree to tree, chasing each other playfully in celebration of the abundance of food that the season provided for the little creatures of town. The spring thaw also lured children outdoors like social ants racing from their colonies on a mission for their queen. The town began a collective stretch to shed its semi-slumber, and the pace of life slowly accelerated as the stiffness of winter was replaced with the vitality of spring.

The energy of Windsor Locks turned frenetic as schools let out for the summer and the town started buzzing like swarms of bees flitting around the thick hedges that bordered our yard. The summer months were hot, but the trees offered shaded respite, and occasional rain showers steamed like a sauna as they cooled the streets.

Windsor Locks is a jewel of small-town America, and I cannot imagine what our lives would have been like had we not grown up there.

Though our little town outwardly boasts the typical New England charm, its greatest treasure is its people. To borrow words from the *Cheers* theme song, it was a town "where everybody knows your name," or at least knew *of* you, especially when the four of us were stumbling through adolescence. With a population of about 10,000 people, it certainly seemed that way.

Our town was filled with modest homes, mostly ranch or Cape Cod-style, occupied by middle-class, blue-collar families, many of whom forged lifelong friendships. While the kids played in well-kept, unfenced yards, our parents hung out and helped each other. A tight-knit community wove through neighborhood after neighborhood, and it wasn't unusual to find us several blocks over, riding our bikes or playing in someone else's yard. Many times, we'd be gone half the day until the glare of streetlights signaled, "Get your butt home right now," and Mom could summon us by issuing a shrill whistle. When we heard it, we knew lollygagging was *not* an option.

The African proverb, "It takes a village to raise a child," perfectly describes our sense of community. The kids knew that no matter where they ventured, *some* pair of adult eyes would be on them, protecting them, but also seeing their mischief. Word of shenanigans got back to parents before the guilty made it home. In the late '70s, Dad bought a three-quarter-ton conversion van with a one-of-a-kind, distinctive exterior. Initially, we thought it was cool but quickly realized everyone knew the Chapman van, so it was difficult to get away with anything. If one of us took it to "Spectator Parking" (a lover's lane of sorts) on either side of the airport, Mom or Dad somehow found out about it. Awkward!

Our neighbor and friend Duane Letendre shared a story about John and the van. It took place after swim practice on a snowy evening when he was a high school junior. Duane, his brother Alan, and John, climbed into the van to drive home. Since the Letendre family lived across the street from us, the boys occasionally hitched a ride with John. The lure of a large, empty parking lot with a slippery layer of newly fallen snow proved too much for John to resist. Duane and Alan hung on for dear life while John spun donuts, sending the heavy van into tight spins, first in one direction and then the other. He sped up and slammed on the brakes to see how far he could slide.

Duane recounted the excitement, "John is one crazy boy! He was doing donuts and got too close to the edge of the parking lot. The van spun around so fast that when it hit the curb, it started to tip over! It was like we were in slow motion. We thought for sure we were going over, but right before we did, the van fell back onto all four tires. We could *not* believe how lucky we were, and all we could do was laugh."

Dad knew about the incident before John walked in the door, but he let it go with nothing more than a warning. John really *was* lucky that night on two fronts.

Being a close-knit town not only facilitated having many eyes upon mischievous kids, but it also cast a protective net over us, allowing the community to watch out for its own, to share in triumphs and tragedies, and to circle the wagons when necessary. Families rallied around each other through suffering and rejoicing. When an F4 tornado blasted down Route 75 without warning in 1979, destroying homes and twisting airplanes at the New England Air Museum into unrecognizable metal pretzels, residents did what they could to help each other. Our house stood less than a mile from the tornado's path of destruction, but we had no idea about the horror unfolding a few blocks away.

Mom had gone to the Finast (short for First National Stores) Supermarket on Route 75 and was taking an inordinately long time. When she finally pulled into the driveway, I went out to help with the groceries and discovered Mom bawling in the driver's seat. Somewhat bewildered, I asked her why she was crying. She could barely speak through her torrent of tears, but blurted out, "You're all ok!"

I hesitated then shook my head in dismay, saying, "Of *course* we're ok. Why wouldn't we be?"

"There was a tornado!" she shrieked.

I stepped back from the van and only then realized that every window was gone; they had imploded into a million pieces all over the interior. Once Dad heard what happened, he left the house, as so many in the town did, to see what assistance he could offer at ground zero of the destruction area. There was no discussion, just an automatic leap into action; like countless cities and towns facing a disaster, it's just what we did.

Sports and other activities proved to be as equally important as adult eyes in keeping us kids out of trouble. The Park Department held summer programs at Pesci Park, including swim lessons in the outdoor pool and arts and crafts on tables nearby. One day, I was doing some crafts while waiting for my swim lesson. Just as I was wrapping up, I felt a warm *splat* on my bare shoulder. A bird had christened me with its poo. I was not too keen on hanging out at the picnic tables after that!

In our teen years, the four of us worked as lifeguards at Pesci Pool and the indoor high school pool. It made perfect sense since we were always at the pool, and we had a blast learning various techniques like jumping off the diving board fully clothed and having to make a flotation device with them.

Along with many of our friends (I swear it was most of the town), we swam for the Windsor Locks Water

Jets, named for what we were most known for—Bradley Airport. We were a very competitive swim team and often hosted AAU (Amateur Athletic Union—an amateur sports organization in the US) meets. They were so much fun; everyone pitched in. Moms sewed little felt animals to sell and brought in baked goods, parents signed up for various meet jobs, and John even played the National Anthem on his accordion. I can still see all of us kids running around, being anxious about our events, and proudly sharing our ribbons. I can smell the pungent chlorine that didn't go away even after a shower. We had perpetually bloodshot eyes until one of the moms read about a solution—drops of milk. It may have been completely psychological, but we were convinced that it worked. At the very least, the cold milk soothed the sting of chlorine.

One by one, we joined the high school teams. Kevin, John, and I didn't only swim; we were also on the dive teams. The boys were so aggressive and fearless; so fun to watch. I was fearless to a point but refused to go past it, especially when I had an exceptionally bad dive during practice. I was trying a front double in the pike position. The boys did it with ease and I wanted to try. It was a great dive until it wasn't. As I snapped out for the entry, I realized it was too soon and ended up crashing onto the surface of the water on my back. It knocked the wind, and my desire to try it again, right out of me! While Kevin and John competed all four years of high school, I faced a tough decision. The girls' team competed in the fall. Our brand-new girls' soccer team also was scheduled for the fall season, so I was forced to choose between my two favorite sports. I chose soccer and my high school swim "career" was over after only one year. The boys went on to set records that endured for many years.

To say we kept busy is an understatement. All four of us joined the Royal Cadets, a marching group that performed in local parades. I twirled the baton while John and Tammy carried the banner at the front of our group. John was also a snare drummer, and Tammy and Kevin occasionally carried a rifle. It was fun *except* our instructor LOVED the song *The Lion Sleeps Tonight*. She played it over and over again during practices. I hate that song to this day!

Besides swimming and the Royal Cadets, we all played soccer, first for the town leagues, and then in high school. John and Kevin played Little League baseball for a few years, but then other activities took priority for them. Tammy and I ran track in high school and I played town league softball. There was no time to get into any trouble, and, yet, we sometimes found it anyway.

To reinforce our sense of right and wrong, and to hopefully keep us out of *big* trouble, Mom brought us to church regularly. Religion played an important role in our home, and we attended St. Robert Bellermine on South Elm Street. Though St. Robert's has undergone renovations over the years, the main building remains as it was so long ago. It is an impressive brick structure reminiscent of a Swiss chalet with a long, sloping roofline that meets at a high peak. A simple cross adorns the large bank of windows that hover over three sets of double doors at the main entrance. To the right of the church is the rectory where Rev. Theodore Raczynski (Father

Ted to his parishioners) and Rev. Thomas Farrell (Father Farrell) lived while they served the people of St. Robert's. Like so many places in town, large, mature hardwoods surround the property, welcoming churchgoers with the soft rustling of leaves.

Our family, minus Dad, attended most every Sunday morning, sitting in the same front-row pew to the left of the altar. Metal hat clips were evenly spaced on the backs of each pew. A few times in our early years, those clips got us into trouble: One or another of us would snap them out of boredom or mischief, drawing stern stares from the pulpit. On the rare occasion that we missed the nonverbal admonishment, our priests let us know in a less subtle way—they paused their sermon and told us to stop. *Then* we got the "stink eye" from Mom.

We all made our First Holy Communions in that church. I took great pride when my turn came in 1973. I felt so grown up in my white dress and veil as I accepted the Eucharist from Father Farrell alongside dozens of other third graders.

Confirmations were held every two years, so John and I were confirmed together. According to AboutCatholics. com, "the sacrament of confirmation is the way for a Catholic to attain full membership in the Catholic Church. It is a beautiful sacrament that will instill God's grace within you to strengthen and sustain you in your journey of faith." John and I were thirteen and fourteen respectively when we were confirmed, so our youthful understanding of confirmation wasn't quite as deep. For us, it signaled that we were viewed as spiritual adults within the church. It was the third of three sacraments—Baptism, First Holy

Communion, and Confirmation—that prepared us for a better understanding of God and the beginning of a close relationship with Him. For us Catholic kids, it was a big deal, and I happily shared it with John.

Each Confirmation candidate chose a sponsor—someone in good standing within the Catholic Church who would commit to making sure their candidate fulfilled his or her sacramental promises. My sponsor was Carolyn (Tersavich) Striniste [now Carolyn Jacobson], a wonderful family friend. John chose Mom. We also had to choose a saint with whom we felt the most aligned and symbolically take his or her name as our own. Apparently, I didn't understand what was being asked of us because I insisted on taking the name Carolyn in honor of my sponsor. There were no saints named Carolyn so, during the confirmation, Archbishop Whelan used a different name! John, on the other hand, at least put a little thought into his choice—Robert, after St. Robert Bellermine.

Church was certainly a big part of our lives—mass every Sunday and every Catholic holiday—but it wasn't always sermons and service. St. Robert's also hosted a bazaar before Christmas so people could sell handmade items. We only went a couple of times, but it was fun to see the talent within our congregation and to, maybe, come away with a small trinket. What we looked forward to most was the annual Strawberry Festival. It was held at a tree-lined plot of land on Southwest Avenue in early summer and most of the town looked forward to it whether they belonged to St. Robert's or not. There were races and track events for kids, small carnival games for prizes, and, *of course*, there were strawberry shortcakes.

The festival has long since stopped, but memories of it still fill me with a childlike happiness.

Our tiny New England town was a wonderful place in which to grow up. It was a tight-knit community that came out in force for its own. The solidarity was never as evident to us as in the days after John was killed. Our dear friend Carolyn immediately went to Mom's house to console her, find a way to ease her pain, and do *something*. She bought dozens of American flags and lovingly placed them in the hedges around the house. People who didn't know us well came by to offer condolences. Our next-door neighbor, who always kept to himself, wrote Mom a beautiful letter, expressing how sorry he was that John was gone. My best friend Lisa (Nolan) Wawruck collected every newspaper article she could find about John and put them in a binder for the future when my emotions weren't so raw. Mom's coworker, Brian Garnett, used to be on the local news, and he volunteered to be her buffer with the press. John had touched so many lives that, through their own shock and grief, the people of Windsor Locks still mobilized around us. It was the caring collective embrace that we so desperately needed.

Though it doesn't seem to be the all-encompassing close-knit community of yesteryear, those friends and families who have been there for decades remain an extraordinary group of people, picking up where their parents left off and becoming the nucleus of the town. And, after two decades, some are still coming up with special ways to honor their hometown hero.

3

Young John—Friends and Compassion

True heroism is remarkably sober, very undramatic.
It is not the urge to surpass all others at
whatever cost, but the urge to serve others
at whatever cost.
~ Arthur Ashe

Dad used to host winter picnics at our house when we were young adults. They didn't happen every year, but he tried to do it as often as possible and continued the tradition after moving back to Michigan. Family and friends came to enjoy Dad's chili and sat around the bonfire, talking, laughing (SO much belly-laughing), and reminiscing. I envisioned doing the same once John retired from the Air Force. I was excited that we would finally get to hear the stories he couldn't share when they were happening. It hurts my heart that there is no chance for his storytelling now so, instead, I invite you to join me at my literary bonfire. Let's roast marshmallows, warm our fingers around a mug of hot chocolate, or hoist a can of Miller Lite® (John's favorite beer) as I regale you with stories about an extraordinary small-town boy.

The first could have ended this book right here. It is the tale of how Kevin and John almost died, and all of the good and goofy things they did after that day never would have happened. In June 1967, when John was almost two years old, he was playing with Kevin and me outside in our little dirt pit. It was a grassless area across the driveway from the back door where we played with Matchbox® cars and Tonka® trucks. I was three-and-a-half and Kevin was five as we *vroom, vroomed* the trucks through the sand.

It began to rain, gently at first, tamping down the dust on our dirt track and creating puddles for our cars to drive through. We were in no hurry to stop playing as the cool rain washed over us. In an instant, the sky grew angry, pelting us with giant raindrops and admonishing us with deafening claps of thunder as lightning lit up our world. It was all the warning I needed. My cars and brothers abandoned, I was already at the door when Mom ran out and shouted for the boys to get inside. As she bent to pick up the toys, she heard an ear-splitting *bang!* Mom turned around to find Kevin and John lying lifelessly on the back steps. A bolt of lightning hit the iron rail they had been holding as they climbed the steps. The charge coursed through the metal and struck the boys with as much force as if the lightning had hit them directly. Mom scooped up their little bodies, ran into the house, and gently laid them down, terrified of what she would discover. To her amazement and profound relief, they were both breathing and eventually came to.

Though they seemed to have come through their ordeal without physical harm, it took several years for John to feel safe during a lightning storm. About a year after the boys had been struck, we were playing outside and it started to thunder. John stood up, screamed at the top of his lungs, and passed out. He repeated that reaction another time when we were at Rainbow Reservoir in Windsor, Connecticut. When a particularly bad thunderstorm rolled through, we couldn't find John anywhere in the house. Mom finally found him under a chair in the living room. There wasn't enough room for him to fit there, but he forced himself into the space anyway. Sweat soaked his little body.

In time, lightning storms no longer affected John. He had somehow overcome his fear, perhaps because he had experienced so many other storms with no bad events and could finally view them without terror.

Remember this story when you start to understand just how many lives John affected over his lifetime. As in the classic Christmas movie, *It's a Wonderful Life*, imagine how things might have gone for so many people had John and Kevin not survived the lightning strike.

From the time John was a young boy, he understood that compassion is powerful; somehow, he understood the importance of putting others before himself. It happened time and again. He decided that everyone should be happy and it was his mission to make it so. John seemed to be in tune with the feelings of everyone around him, especially Mom, and he tried to comfort her even when he was so young he could barely talk. Mom remembers, "If he sensed I was sad or upset, he cupped my face, saying, 'It's ok, Mommy.'"

At the tender age of five, John and his kindergarten class went on a field trip to The Institute for American Indian Studies in Washington, Connecticut. In keeping with tradition, Mom gave him a couple of dollars to spend at the favorite stop of any school outing—the gift shop. Unlike every other child there that day, John didn't buy himself a meaningless trinket to be cast aside the instant he brought it home. Instead, he chose a tiny oil lamp. It was four-and-a-half inches tall, clear glass with swirls of red and blue, and it probably cost him every penny. John gingerly carried it home, his excitement barely contained, and raced into the living room where he thrust it into Mom's outstretched hands. She was floored. It was a gesture she would never forget, and a treasure she would forever keep. She has it on a shelf in her living as a reminder of her little boy's giving heart.

Brian Topor was on the field trip too. He lived on Jackson Street, a short walk from our house, and he became one of John's best friends for life. During their years at Southwest Elementary School, Brian occasionally came to our house in the morning so he and John could continue walking to school together. Brian remembers, "I recall that when we met up, we greeted each other with an affectionate jolt to the arm. We would then find a pebble, or a piece of ice in the wintertime, and kick it all the way to school. I don't recall engaging in much conversation during those times, but I know that I always enjoyed his company."

Outside of walking to and from school, John and Brian were often joined by David Wrabel, another lifelong friend, and it wasn't unusual for the three friends to be seen running around the neighborhood, playing hide-and-seek, or tag. Sometimes, they played "Army," and it was their dream to be Green Berets and become heroes. Of course, none had ever heard of Air Force Combat Control or, as Brian later said, they might have aspired to be that instead.

Over a decade after John's death, Brian, David, and another childhood friend Mike Toce reminisced about going to his funeral and meeting those in his "other life;" his other brotherhood. Brian said, "The neatest part was, even though they're just ordinary people, they're extraordinary in what they do." The friends were getting a glimpse into the kind of guys they were—the kind of guy John had been. David laughed, "I was amazed by the things they had to do. In my job, the biggest hazard was a paper cut."

Back when the little boys were playing "Army," I'm sure none of them thought for even a moment that one of them would actually do it in real life … only better. John was an Air Force Combat Controller.

When we moved to Windsor Locks, our family became very close with neighbors two doors down on Cornwall Drive. Howie and Evelyn Tersavich and their seven children quickly became more like family than just friends. We celebrated birthdays and other occasions at one house or the other, and we even vacationed together a few times in New Hampshire. We spent hot afternoons at People's Forest in Barkhamsted, Connecticut, playing ball in the open fields, eating burgers and delicious homemade food, and floating down the Farmington River on inner tubes. One time, I was tubing with Skeeter, the youngest Tersavich who is Kevin's age, and we decided to see how far we could float. We ended up miles down the river, exiting into someone's backyard, and sinking up to our shins in slimy muck. To top it off, we then had to hoof it those extra miles back to the picnic area! We were barefoot and quickly realized we had not thought out the trip very well. Nevertheless, I still remember it fondly because it was fun (but not enough to do again).

During the summer of 1980, our families went to Spofford Lake in Chesterfield, New Hampshire. Mr. T, as we called him, owned a boat, and some of his kids took turns water skiing behind it. None of us had skied before, so we were excited to see how it was done. Eventually, I was able to get up and ski on two skis and it was exhilarating—until I received a massive wedgie when I wiped out!

John had been watching Skeet as he skied like a pro. John was intrigued, but what caught his attention most was Skeet's ability to ski on one ski, and he wanted to do it. Skeet taught him to get up on two skis and then drop one after he was up and stable. John conquered that maneuver immediately. It wasn't challenging enough. He marveled as Skeet got up using only one ski and then circled the lake. *That* was the challenge he wanted, and he made up his mind to do it too. Honest to God, it only took him one or two tries and he was up and skiing on one ski! Only *then* was he satisfied that he had pushed himself enough.

I remain close with Skeet and, as we talked about John one random day, he chuckled at a memory from long ago.

> The number one story that always sticks in my mind was the time he bit my inner thigh when I had his arms and Kevin had his legs. He was probably five or six years old tops, maybe younger. He was wrestling to get out of it, and the best thing he could come up with was latching onto my thigh. Well, it worked because I dropped him. After he bit me, I ran home crying and pulled my pants down to see the upper and lower teeth marks that he left behind. It hurt so much; I'll never forget it—the right inner thigh. I was back at your house within the hour playing again. When I told my mother that I was going back, she said, 'What happened to never playing with him again?' He left no scars, but it's proof he was a fighter from a young age. That story is always near and dear to my heart.

Why does this story not surprise me? Settle in and you'll discover why as I share more stories.

Unlike his friendship with Skeet, John's friendship with Billy Brooks only lasted during their school years, but it was a devotion that changed the course of Billy's life. As a new kid in town in 1970, Billy got off to a rough start on the very first day of kindergarten. He remembers, "I must have said something to irritate Maureen Walsh, and she punched me in the stomach. I dropped to my knees, holding my middle and thinking in my five-year-old brain, 'First day of kindergarten. This isn't going good.' Then a boy stepped in front of me and held up his hands as if to say, 'Hold on here.'"

The boy was John and, although he was also only five, he understood that the new kid needed help, so he stepped in when the rest of the kindergarteners had no idea what to do. Their friendship grew stronger in middle school, where Billy was an incredibly shy boy, unable to talk to *anyone*. His shyness, coupled with his physique ("I was a rolly polly kid."), made him uncomfortable in his own skin. John accepted him as he was and, with more than a little encouragement, he eventually started to realize that others could too.

Shyness followed Billy as they started high school in 1979, but, with John by his side, things slowly began to change. They had lunch together every day, and, even though John also spent time with other friends, he never made Billy feel like he didn't matter. When he and John were in French class together during their junior year, he was still apprehensive about talking to people. Their teacher planned a trip to Quebec, Canada, to practice the language and experience a French community. They were going with a group of girls from Penny High School in East Hartford, and there was no way Billy was going— no way, no how. John had other plans. He decided there was no way, no how Billy *wouldn't* go. He nudged him, "Come on! Why wouldn't you go?" and he kept nudging until Billy caved; he would go *only* if John went too.

They stuck together throughout their entire French-Canadian adventure, and, when John found out Billy wanted to ask one of the girls to the prom, he was excited for him. Billy was still convinced he could never talk to anyone, *especially* a girl, so he balked. John pushed back, "Come on, just ask her." He persisted until Billy finally thought, "John is right. Why *can't* I do this?" Trembling inside, he asked Kim Culcasi to the prom, and, to his amazement, she said, "Yes!" Billy gives credit to John that he and Kim are now lifelong friends. Had he not pushed Billy just far enough out of his comfort zone, had he not said, "At least just ask," the friendship between Billy and Kim probably would not have happened. She was the first person he called when he found out John had died.

With John as leader of a faction of the field-trippers, they decided to ditch their chaperone and teacher, "Papa" Labrosse, to see what mischief the Quebec nightlife offered. There were five or six girls and about as many guys, including John and Billy, and they hatched a plan to sneak out of the hotel one night. They couldn't go past the front desk, so the clever teens used the fire escape that was outside the room that John and Billy occupied. One after the other, they climbed out the window, the last one propping it open so they could sneak back in when their galivanting was done. As they quietly descended the metal stairs and approached the window below, they remembered that Papa Labrosse's room was directly below John's! Those who were already outside Papa's window froze, terrified he would see them and imagining their punishment for the attempted breakout. As they peered into his window, they realized he wasn't moving and someone whispered, "Hey, I think he's passed out!"

The rowdy bunch ended up on the lively streets of Quebec for a few hours, traipsing into one place after another, high on adrenaline over ditching their chaperone. Around three in the morning, the wayward group tottered back to the hotel, fully intending on climbing the fire escape in reverse of their exit. Instead, fueled by liquid courage, they found enough bravery to stagger right past the front desk. The clerk could not have cared less, and Papa Labrosse never discovered their shenanigans.

Their return to school was probably a drag for most, but not for Billy. His adventure gave him a new-found confidence that may never have happened had he not gone to Quebec with John.

After high school, Bill graduated from the *Culinary Institute of America* in Hyde Park, New York, and went on to be a Corporate Chef at US Foods. He travels the world, speaking in front of groups, and is convinced that he would not be where he is today had it not been for John's friendship and encouragement.

I met with Bill in September 2016 and asked if he was surprised by John's actions on the day he died. He immediately responded:

> None of it surprises me. Not even a little bit. I don't know if he even knew he was helping me all those years ago, but he helped me get to where I am now. When I first heard the news that John had

died, I just had to pause, thinking, "Wait a minute. I haven't spoken to him since we walked out the doors of Windsor Locks High." And that seemed to be the way we were from the time I first met him; we kind of went in and out of each other's lives, but the times that he came back into my life were the times that I *needed* him there. I can't imagine how my life would have been without John in it.

I often wonder, as Bill did, whether John was ever aware of how much he was affecting someone's life at the time it was happening, or even *that* he made a difference. I imagine, in his mind, he was just being a friend.

One of John's most endearing stories of friendship revolves around Mary Tersavich. She was Skeet's sister, the fourth of the Tersavich seven, and when Mom and Dad bought the house two doors away, John was one year old. Mary was twelve and wheelchair-bound because of a doctor's tragic miscalculation ten years earlier. Mary had been left with brain damage, which resulted in her being quadriplegic. Though physically disabled and mentally diminished, Mary had a memory like a steel trap, never forgetting a thing she saw or a promise made to her. Physical activity was limited to lying on the floor to color with a pencil she held in her mouth. All of us kids loved her like a sister, but Tammy and John were the ones who always made sure to spend the most time with her. When she was little, Tammy liked to climb up Mary's wheelchair to sit in her lap and give kisses. Many times, as the rest of us were playing outside, John chose to stay inside with Mary, coloring beside her on the floor, talking quietly, and switching out her pencils when she wanted a new color. Mom took a photo one of those times—her twelve-year-old boy choosing Mary over everyone else.

As an adult, John continued to shower Mary with love every time he came to town. He "danced" with her at a family wedding, twirling her wheelchair around and "dipping" her backward. He even pulled her out of the chair so she could dance upright, holding her tightly as she laughed with absolute glee.

John brought his wife and daughters to meet her on his few trips home. Mary's love for John was so powerful that she always imagined she would marry him, even after he married Valerie; it was something she thought was *supposed* to happen. Mary understood that John was gone and her heart broke over losing her sweetheart. She kept a photo of him on the wall across from her bed right up until the day she died. Sweet Mary passed away in July 2022 and is now twirling around a Heavenly dance floor with John, light on her feet and giddy with joy, all while being serenaded by her other lifelong crush Glen Campbell.

John's compassion wasn't only reserved for humans, he also had a heart for animals. One hot summer afternoon when he was ten, John was sitting on a giant wooden electrical cord spool eating a peanut butter sandwich when he heard a scratching noise behind him. He turned to find a squirrel sitting a foot away. Ever so slowly, he offered a piece of his lunch by placing it on the spool just inches in front of her. She ate it quickly, eyeing him intently. After making short work of her morsel, she looked up as if to ask, "That's it?" He repeatedly broke off more pieces and left them closer and closer to himself until she finally took them from his outstretched fingers.

John got to name her since she approached him first, and he came up with Mrs. S. It may not be the most creative name, but he was ten! Though John was quickly able to feed her by hand, as each of us tried, she had to be coaxed to understand we wouldn't hurt her either. She was a smart little squirrel, quickly learning that, if she showed up and waited, one of us would head out to feed her the sunflower seeds that Mom felt compelled to buy for our "pet."

Mrs. S eventually felt comfortable enough to crawl all over us. She even brought her offspring to meet us every spring, and we looked forward to seeing her. Some of them would cautiously take food from our hands and dart away, but none were as bold as she. We kept their food just inside the back door, and she knew it. On one occasion, when we weren't home, she decided to help herself by biting through the screen and dropping in for a meal. Weeks later, Dad and I were scraping wallpaper in the living room when we heard a soft *tick, tick, tick* coming from the kitchen. I peeked around the corner and spied Mrs. S casually tiptoeing across the floor like she owned the place. We chased her out of the hole in the screen. Mom was not happy when we told her, so she devised a plan. She picked up the bag of seeds, brought it outside, and showed it to Mrs. S. She then held it in full view as she walked to the shed, being sure Mrs. S saw her put it inside. From that day on, we never had an unexpected dinner guest chew her way into the house; she waited by the shed.

Our wild "pet" came to visit us for many years; Mom thinks it was about five. One spring, she showed up looking as though she had survived a fight, her eye crusted over from the injury, and we realized there would come a day that she wouldn't come back. It happened a year or two later. Whether she died of old age or fell victim to a predator or vehicle, we were sad when she stopped coming around. We held fast to the thought that, had John not befriended her, we would never have known a smart and friendly little squirrel named Mrs. S.

4

Mom's Little Rascal

I believe in kindness. Also in mischief.
~ Mary Oliver

John's level of compassion exceeded his age and the times. It was something he gave freely to anyone he thought needed it. But even though John was a compassionate boy, he also had a *very* strong mischievous streak that usually began with a sparkle in his brilliant blue eyes. He greatly appreciated the value of light-hearted shenanigans and, at times, mischievous mayhem. He was clever and brazen but never mean-spirited, and many of his escapades resulted in countless moments of belly laughs and uncontrollable giggles. Oh, the mischief John could find! He has always been Mom's Little Rascal.

Great Grandma Kennedy—we called her Granny— lived with our grandparents in New Jersey. To us kids, she was gruff, kind of mean, and more than a little strange. We didn't know until years later that she was schizophrenic; all we knew was that she was *not* pleasant, and we sometimes took it as a license to be devilish in return. It was mostly just harmless fun, like when we threw something attached to a string into the living room in front of her, then slowly pulled it back. Her hearing and eyesight were awful, so she couldn't see the string, just the object moving by itself. We thought it was hilarious.

Once a year, Granny stayed with us for two weeks so Grandma and Grandpa could go on vacation. Mom always offered *my* bed to her and, every time, I thought, "Yay! I get to sleep in the living room." It never happened. Instead of being liberated from the Granny trap, I had to sleep in Tammy's bed while *she* got the enviable privilege of sleeping on the couch. That's how it went for several years, and John listened intently as I complained about having to give up my bed *and* stay in the room with Granny. It was the same story every time: "I'm always in bed before Granny comes into the room, and even if I pretend to be asleep, she tells me to face the wall while she gets dressed for bed."

She wore a corset that *had* to have at least a million hooks and, for a young child forced to stay still for any amount of time, it was pure torture waiting for those damn corset hooks to be undone. I couldn't help but count in my head, "One. Two. Three. Four." Would she *ever* get through all of those stupid hooks?! Tears *always* came. It was pure torture, and during every visit, I complained to whoever I could corner that "it took for-ev-er for Granny to get through the million hooks and *then* it took her for-ev-er to get ready for bed." John hung on every word; very curious about what Granny could possibly be doing that had me facing the wall for an eternity every night.

When John was six and she came for her stay, the routine started. I went to bed, trying to fall asleep before

Granny came into the room, but noooo! She did her slow shuffle down the hall before sleep could save me from the torture of what came next. It was the second night of Granny's visit, and John had already heard my sob story from the night before. Shortly after Granny entered the room, closing the door as slowly as cold molasses, Mom heard muffled giggling coming from the end of the hall. "I knew immediately who it was; there was no mistaking it." Mom pressed an ear to the door and heard John's unmistakable laugh, which was more like a cackle when he thought something was really funny. She knew her little rascal was at it again. She whispered loudly, "Johnny, are you in the girls' bedroom?"

While I pretended to be asleep, he giggled again, and Mom told him to get out of there. He waited for his moment, then scurried from under Tammy's bed and ran into the hall cackling. He told Mom quite matter-of-factly, "I wanted to find out what Granny does that takes so long." John had planned ahead, making entry into my room, and hiding under the bed before Granny made her way in at her turtle pace. She never knew he was there; never heard Mom's whispers or John's cackling. He even made his escape without her realizing what had happened. Holding back her own laughter, Mom scolded him and sent him off to bed again. He was disappointed that he hadn't been under the bed long enough to discover "the big Granny secret," and it wouldn't be the last time he got away with doing something I would never have dared.

41

Our childhood was rife with pranks like John's Granny story, but there were times when his shenanigans were borne out of defiance. When Mom sent us to our rooms for punishment, we frequently languished for a long time because she would forget she put us there. John occasionally liberated himself from forgotten lockdown. He bragged to me after one breakout, and of course it pissed me off. That kid never got caught! Maybe I was just jealous because it never even occurred to me to defy Mom, and even if it had, I'd have been too chicken to try. I was secretly impressed.

One sunny afternoon, ten-year-old John was ordered into solitary confinement and immediately climbed out of his window, hightailed it to the large pine tree at the front corner of our house, and reveled in his clever escape. The pine branches reached around each side of the corner, creating a cave between the house and the tree trunk. The outside branches went all the way to the ground so no one could see there was a cavity behind it. John played with his Matchbox® cars until he figured he had been gone about an hour or so. He returned to the window, climbed back in, and went to bed. He laughed, "Not long after laying down, Mom came in, all upset because she forgot about me being in there." Been *there*, done *that*.

Tammy remembers John making his escape another way. Dad framed a hole in the floor of our bathroom linen closet so we could throw our dirty clothes into the basement. It wasn't very big—maybe twelve inches square. John slipped out the door to his room and scooted across the narrow hall into the bathroom. From there, he shimmied down the hole, opened one of the small basement windows, and climbed to freedom that way. The spider webs around the basement windows would have kept me away! When John was on a mission, nothing stood in his way, not even spiders.

To say that he loved mischief is a huge understatement. John found some sort of tomfoolery almost every day, but not all of his mischief went according to plan. Sometimes things went a little sideways, and the intended outcome failed miserably. Over the years, some of that harmless fun went undetected, but there *were* times he had to correct a miscalculation.

When John was nine years old, he and Kevin thought it would be funny to put little Patty Dixon's bicycle up into their maple tree and leave it there, only they were not satisfied with keeping it low. They dragged it as high as they could, into the smallest, weakest branches. The boys didn't do it to be mean; they just thought it was a really funny prank. Had it not been for the Dixon's next-door neighbor, the bike might not have been found for quite some time. He saw something flashing in the sunlight and told Mr. Dixon. Once they figured out that it was Patty's missing bicycle, Mr. Dixon tried to retrieve it, but he had to stop far short of the small upper branches and the bike that beckoned just out of reach. Patty couldn't have been more than six years old, and she was traumatized by seeing her bike hanging high in the tree. Tammy found out how upset Patty was and, unaware that her brothers were the culprits, she told John that Patty was crying about her bike. John's secret delight over their clever prank disintegrated. He had to make it right.

His sense of honor became evident to Mrs. Dixon when she opened her door to a sorrowful little boy. He went to their house on his own and made a full confession. He wanted to fix it, knowing full well that trouble most assuredly awaited him. No one suspected Kevin or him; he could have stayed quiet and none would have been the wiser. But his heart couldn't accept the pain that their caper had caused Patty, so he apologized to her and climbed the tree to undo the prank. Mr. and Mrs. Dixon were impressed that John had taken responsibility, and they didn't tell Mom and Dad—not until after he was killed. Maryanne Dixon felt compelled to tell the story of unexpected compassion and honesty from Mom's little rascal. At a memorial for John in an Air National Guard hangar, she sought Mom out and shared her pride in one little boy—mother-to-mother.

The Dixon incident ended better than John expected, but he didn't always fess up to his mischief. There were times when he just did something naughty, plain and simple. In his mid-teens, when Kevin became very interested in ninja stars and throwing knives, he ordered some through a catalog. This was long before the Internet, so where he even found that kind of catalog is beyond me. He was obsessed with them for a time and even got caught with one in his shirt pocket as he went through the metal detector at the airport! As a United Airlines employee, Dad was *not* happy. Kevin knew better but, he, too, enjoyed some antics. The ninja stars gave John a devious idea. One evening, he "borrowed" some, ferreted them away in his rolled-up towel, and hid them in his locker before swim practice at the high school. Afterward, John and a friend (name withheld to protect the guilty) thought it would be fun to throw the stars at the inside of the locker room door. Their target was heavy and solid—over an inch thick—and it held up wonderfully against their assaults. Since most of the kids left through the other side of the locker room, the odds of detection were low. John and his friend stippled the inside of the door with gouges too numerous to count.

Mom is certain the boys were never caught, nor did they "turn themselves in." She asserted, "If they *had* been caught, we [the parents] would have been notified, and I'm sure they would have had to sand the indentations, or pay for a new door, or something. I didn't find out until years later." Tammy confirmed the story, so how do we know of it? Either one of them developed loose lips or, more probable, John may have told us long after it happened. I *can* say this: That scarred door remained as the entrance to the boys' locker room for years. Mom and I visited in October 2002 and were astonished to see it still there—battle scars and all. For those who wondered about the pockmarked door in years past, wonder no longer. It was John and his mystery accomplice.

John was generally a good kid with a kind heart and a sense of right and wrong, but not always. As established, he was also mischievous and annoying. When they were in their mid-teens, John decided to follow Kevin one day, but not from a distance. He was so close Kevin felt John's breath on his neck. He went everywhere Kevin did, right behind him, pestering him, knowing it was pissing him off. When he had had enough of his antagonist, Kevin darted into their room, scooped up their plastic garbage can, and swung it backward as hard as he could. It hit the wall with such force that it caved in the drywall. John stopped, looked at the indentation, and got the message. There were no more antics that day.

He wasn't the only one with a knack for irritation; we all had our moments. We pestered and angered each other, most times over idiotic stuff, but once one of us "tapped out," that was the end. Ok, *usually* that was the end. Sometimes, the poking persisted until we elicited the desired response. It was all fun and games until someone got hurt or pissed. Siblings are supposed to annoy each other, aren't we?

5

The Family Comedian

*There is a certain happiness in being
silly and ridiculous.*
~ Unknown

Forgive me, Mom. I have to share this story. There is
mischief, and there is pure silliness. What could be sillier
than farts? The mere mention of the word brings a chuckle
to many people if they're bold enough to admit it. John
knew the value of perfectly timed flatulence; it was comic
relief for a stressful situation, or just an opportunity to elicit
feigned disgust and nose-pinched laughter. We learned our
"fartitude" from Dad, who also never let an opportunity
pass without putting forth an effort, but John took it to a
whole new level. At a young age, he taught himself to fart
on command, and I will let your imagination lead you to
how he did it. He held it a few seconds, waiting for the
right moment, and then let loose. Farting for effect was
absolutely *not* something Mom encouraged; I must make
that clear. Heck, farting in general wasn't acceptable.
She was not amused, so John usually didn't deploy his
obnoxious skill if she was around.

One night, John's unique talent brought a new and unexpected element of surprise. He might have been eight, so I was nine. Mom and Dad were out, and Kevin was as in charge as he could be of siblings not much younger than himself. When we were alone, antics usually started small and escalated as we egged each other on. We were all running around in our pajamas, playing jokes on each other, and doing whatever we could imagine to delay bedtime. Mom and Dad were only gone a couple of hours, but that was plenty of time for us to ramp up the silliness instead of going to bed.

We were screeching and tearing around when John chased me into the bathroom, and I was trapped. He decided that his singular captive audience needed a sampling of his particular skillset, so he assumed the position and made ready. I stood next to the tub, waiting for him to release so I could pretend to be grossed out. John made his "fart-release" grimace and let it go. We started giggling immediately, but, just as quickly, John's expression turned to surprise—pure and utter shock. He straightened up and said, "Oh no." He jiggled his left leg vigorously and, from the bottom of his loose pajama pants, a tiny ball of poop landed with a soft plop onto the floor. I let out a girly scream and our giggles turned into belly laughs as I ran past him, hugging the wall and cutting as wide a path around that little turd as possible in the tiny bathroom. By the time I escaped, I was laughing so hard my legs were rubbery and gave way as I dropped to the living room floor. I was unable to retreat any farther, and I heard John's unmistakable cackle coming from the bathroom as he took care of business. We laughed so hard our stomachs hurt.

"Never a dull moment" so accurately describes John; it didn't matter what we were doing. Dad used to take the boys fishing, and the night before an outing, we all went "night crawling" to look for worms. I hated fishing, but the worm hunts were lots of fun. We would lie on the ground, searching for the live bait that would, hopefully, attract big fish. Being quick was key because, if our prey sensed us ready to pounce, it immediately disappeared into the soft, damp earth. John was in seventh grade when we drove to the middle school to hunt for large, juicy night crawlers. It was one of our favorite hunting spots. With only two flashlights, we relied on the lights at the back of the school. We were getting ready to leave when John lay down on a cement doorstep. His head hovered beyond the edge as the light from above cast a shadow over the area in front of him. He startled us when he yelled, "I found one! It's *HUGE*!" John inched forward gingerly as he stalked his quarry, quickly descending upon it to ensure there was no chance of escape. He smashed his hand upon the juicy victim and raised his arm in victory. Glee immediately turned to disgust when he realized his prize wasn't a worm at all; it was a piece of dog poop! While John furiously wiped his hand on the dewy grass, the rest of us laughed hysterically. John didn't cackle *that* night, but he did chuckle a little. Not all of John's antics involved excrement or flatulence, I swear! Sometimes he was just funny.

In our pre-adolescent years, if we got into trouble with Mom, she sometimes uttered those six dreaded words, "Wait 'til your father comes home." We hoped against hope she'd forget by the time he came home from work, but our prayers for cosmic intervention never worked. If the transgression was so egregious to evoke that warning, we knew "the belt" was in our very near future. We listened from the other room as Mom recounted the story of our misdeed to Dad. The awful sound of his belt slithering from its loops came next. He folded it in half and snapped it loudly for effect. The anticipation was almost more painful than the lashing itself. Once we were primed for punishment, the dance began. Dad grasped the upper left arm to keep us from escaping, and, as he swung the belt onto our behinds, we involuntarily popped up onto our tippy-toes and pranced around in a circle, all the while being chased by the lethal leather. He didn't beat the tar out of us, but it was enough for us to get the message with stings to our pride *and* to our cheeks.

By the time John was eight, he had endured enough belt licks to know how much it hurt, so he formulated a scheme as he waited for punition one day. It was a simple and brilliant plan to outwit Dad, or at least *he* thought it was. John stepped up with confidence to take his punishment, probably giggling inside over his cunning. The belt landed on his butt with a *thud* instead of a slap. He had shoved a thin paperback book into his underwear to absorb the sting, and, if that didn't work, *surely* Dad

50

would think it was funny and he'd be spared altogether. It was ingenious! Sadly, Dad didn't think it was clever or funny. John was aghast over his failure as he slowly removed the book, knowing what came next—more licks than he would have received otherwise. Knowing Dad, he had to have been at least a little impressed with John's ingenuity, but there was no way he could let it eliminate the punishment.

John loved new experiences, from strange concoctions in the kitchen to jumping off cliffs, and he did them all with great exuberance. The most ordinary thing could elicit excitement, especially when he was young.

In the spring of 1973, eight-year-old John was excited to start his first year of Little League baseball. He had all of his equipment except one that he couldn't do without—the one designed to protect his tender family jewels. Dad brought him to Scott's Sports Supplies in Windsor and bought his very first jockstrap and cup. John had never seen anything like it! There was nothing but straps to hold it on and a pouch for the gems. Once home, he was so curious about his new sports contraption that he *had* to take it on a test run. He raced into his room with the Scott's bag swinging wildly in his hand and slammed the door behind him.

The boys' bedroom had two doors because it was originally meant to be a dining room—one door led to the kitchen and the other to the hall on the other side of the living room. We could run a circle from their room, through the kitchen, into the living room, and back into their room, and there were countless chases 'round and 'round over the years. On this particularly comical day, John put on his little boy jock strap—and nothing else! He flung open the door, pausing for dramatic effect, then streaked the kitchen/living room loop twice all while giggling hysterically and yelling, "Funny undies! Funny undies!"

Who knew jock straps could be so entertaining?

As much as John's humor was usually well-received, there *were* occasions when his antics cost him dearly -- like at the end of 7th grade. Brian Topor and John were in gym class; the days were numbered until summer break and the two of them developed a tendency to be a little "vocal" to the wrong person, their gym teacher and soccer coach. They also did things in gym that got them in trouble, like kicking the ball up to the gym ceiling. Coach yelled at them and the boys laughed. He called them, "Wise guys," pronouncing it *wice gice* and misting them with spittle. John wiped his face with a towel right in front of him, eliciting more laughter from Brian. They *were* wise guys, and Coach said they would not be able to play soccer the following year because of their actions.

The next year came and they probably didn't even remember Coach's threat. John and Brian went to soccer tryouts and, true to his word, the coach did not let either of them play. They were off the team for their 8th grade season. That was a high price to pay, but the lesson was not lost on either of them.

6

Promises, Promises

*Promise is one thing. Fulfilling that
promise is quite another.*
~ Alex Ferguson

John was a man of his word. Honor, integrity, perseverance, and determination—he had them all and more. If he committed to something, he took the promise seriously and, if needed, would move heaven and earth to get it done. Even as a little boy, John understood that earning trust meant putting others first; and pushing to complete a pledge. Lip service was not an option for him.

When John was eight years old and in third grade, he asked Mom if he could take accordion lessons. A company had visited the school to demonstrate instruments, and John was fascinated with the accordion. Money was usually tight in the Chapman household, so Mom told John she would have to talk with Dad first. She liked that John wanted to play the accordion because, though she had never heard him play it, her own father had once tickled the ivories and bass buttons of the complicated instrument. It would be fun to watch John do something her dad had also enjoyed.

The cost of accordion lessons wasn't exorbitant, but it still impacted the budget, so Mom made a deal with John, "You have to take lessons for at least four years, and you have to practice at least an hour every day." He agreed to the terms and stuck to it, practicing diligently every day for an hour. Kevin, Tammy, and I did not appreciate his dedication because he had to practice either in the kitchen or the living room—right where the rest of us were. Our loud complaints never swayed John. He practiced every day and even got to play the occasional *Star Spangled Banner* at important special events. He also didn't care that it wasn't considered the "coolest" instrument; he grew quite proficient for his age and just loved playing it.

He did have his admirers though. Childhood friend Rob LaBreche vividly remembers, "I was at his birthday party at your house, and he played it. I was so damn jealous at the time; he actually made playing the accordion cool for maybe the first time in history. Cool to me at least."

David Wrabel echoed that sentiment in his eulogy at John's funeral.

> I remember going over to John's house; we were probably shooting soccer balls, and, after some time, we went into the house to get something to drink. The next thing I see is John carrying a big box and out comes an accordion. I'm not quite sure what [song] he played, but I vividly remember the accordion was bigger than John, and it almost fell

to the ground as he attempted to fill the bellows with air. It truly was quite a sight.

In time, John's instructor told Mom that he could be exceptional but would have to concentrate almost solely on accordion. She knew that wouldn't happen because John also loved his sports and other activities. She was content with how he was doing, and his instructor was happy that John met all of his requirements. He did so well in his first year of lessons that his instructor signed him up for a competition. He placed second.

The day finally came, though, when John was twelve years old and said, "Mom, I don't have any time to be a little boy anymore." When Mom asked what he meant, he quietly replied, "Well, I have music, and soccer, and swim team, and school, and homework. I don't have much time to play and stuff." She listened and then said, "Ok, you choose what you want to stop. Do you want to stop one of your sports teams or the music . . . " and he interrupted, "Would you care if I stop taking lessons? I'll still play but not take lessons anymore and not have to practice." Mom was proud of her then not-so-little boy and she agreed, "You fulfilled your promise. You did a good job."

Four years of accordion lessons and daily one-hour practices: Promise kept.

★ ★ ★ ★

Swimming was one of the activities John did not want to sacrifice for the accordion. He had been on the town swim team since he was six and wasn't willing to give it up. His dedication to the sport started early. In 1973, the high school pool hosted a fifty-lap swim to benefit the March of Dimes. John was eight years old and decided he wanted to do it, promising to finish the fifty laps. As he gathered pledges from people, most offered five or ten cents per lap, all probably figuring he would complete only a few laps. One of his pledges came from a business owner who pledged a dollar a lap. Mom was concerned and told Dad, "You better go tell him to reassess his thinking. Johnny will finish his fifty laps." Dad went back to the man and said, "You realize that this is going to cost you $50," and the guy's mouth dropped open. He was sure a little boy would only do one or two laps, so he had been fine with paying a higher amount per lap. He thanked Dad and lowered his pledge but still ended up being the highest contributor to the little Chapman boy.

The youngest swimmer to participate in the fundraiser, John started his fifty laps by swimming the butterfly stroke for the first couple of laps. He quickly realized it took too much energy to maintain that difficult stroke, so for the rest of the swim, he alternated between backstroke and breaststroke. He promised Mom, "I'm gonna do them all. I'm not going to stop and rest in between." True to his word, John finished all fifty laps without stopping. Promise kept, and of all the swimmers participating in the fundraiser, he raised the most money as an individual.

John's determination as a swimmer didn't end at the fundraiser. One summer, he went to an AAU meet at the swim area of the Globe Hollow Reservoir in

Manchester, Connecticut. They had lanes set up, but the thought of swimming without the walled boundaries of a pool freaked John out a little. He was in the eight-and-under age group, which usually swam twenty-five yards for events. For this meet, though, the kids had to swim fifty yards: twenty-five yards to a floating platform and twenty-five yards back. John and his friend Monica were slated to swim butterfly in their events, and, as they surveyed the lake, neither was sure they could do it. During a lunch break, they decided to swim it on their own. Both completed the full fifty yards and learned they had nothing to fear. John and Monica each won medals that day because they were determined and willing to "test the waters." This time it was a promise to himself: "I promise to try. I promise to do my best." And he did.

This story has played out over and over again throughout John's life. Determination, preparation, confidence, and sometimes sheer grit, got John through many situations, including most of his last one. He was a boy/man of his word to the very end. Before leaving for Afghanistan, he told Tammy, "I will do anything in my power to protect my team." He fulfilled that promise with his life.

7

Life Lessons and Dad's Unique Approach to Them

*The most valuable lessons in life cannot be taught,
they must be experienced.*
~ Liam Payne

Dad sometimes found some pretty slick ways of teaching life lessons, many of which stuck with us long into adulthood. We did not appreciate some of his tactics when they were happening, but we came away with experience.

When Dad was growing up in Michigan, he hunted in the winter months with his father, learning survival skills and hunting techniques. Those were lessons he wanted to pass on to Kevin and John. Tunxis Forest surrounds Barkhamsted Reservoir in north central Connecticut and borders the Granville State Forest in Massachusetts. It is a half-hour drive from our home and was the location for the boys' winter camping weekends. They camped two or three years in a row—one in February 1975 when John was ten. Mom dropped them off at a designated spot along the road in Hartland, and they disappeared into the woods, trudging through snow that sometimes measured four feet deep and carrying minimal survival gear in their packs: an axe, shovel, matches, sleeping bags, and some plastic.

Kevin chronicled some of their winter camping exploits in a short paper he wrote in high school. Dad taught them to build a lean-to shelter using rope and small logs for the frame and pine boughs for roofing. Their shelter wasn't pretty, but it accomplished the task. They also used the pine boughs under the sleeping bags to insulate against the cold snow beneath. In order to reflect heat from the campfire and to protect against ashes being blown into the shelter, Dad had the boys build a firewall by driving small logs into the snow. They gathered firewood, built a campfire, cooked strips of steak, and spent the nights huddled together in the lean-to.

One morning, they packed up and hiked through the snow for about an hour to the base of a small cliff about twenty feet high. Kevin wrote, "There was a path that wound up the cliff and a deer path that went around it." Dad and John took the deer path and Kevin decided to go up the cliff path. He scaled the cliff easily but faced steep, icy ground up the hill. There were sharp rocks at the base of the cliff below, so he climbed carefully, slipped, caught himself, and continued. When he could finally rest, he reached into his pockets and discovered one of his gloves was missing. It taunted him from halfway down the slope. Kevin dropped his pack and crept slowly down the icy hill.

He wrote:
Just as I was bending over to pick up the glove, I slipped again. This time I couldn't stop. There

wasn't much to grab hold to. The first ten feet weren't bad, but after that, I was sliding pretty fast. I was frantically trying to dig my hands into the ice. I saw a tree coming up and lunged for it but missed. Doing so twisted my body sideways. After that, I gave up hope of trying to save myself and prayed that God would save me. He did. Just as I was nearing the edge, two trees stopped me.

Those trees were really nothing more than small saplings, but they were enough to keep Kevin from flying off the edge and onto the rocks below. What are the odds?

Most fathers did not take their sons (or daughters) winter survival camping, but Dad wasn't "most fathers." There is no doubt that Kevin and John learned some valuable lessons and acquired survival skills from their camping trips. They also came away with some pretty entertaining stories!

When I say Dad came up with some unique ways of teaching us, I'm not kidding. And some of them were infuriating. We used to go hiking in the mountains of Connecticut and Massachusetts, and, after a while, I would start zoning out—not paying attention to what was going on around me. On one outing, I hit the zone and kept hiking. When I snapped out of it, I realized I was all alone in the middle of the woods. My family was nowhere to be found. After walking around a bit and calling out to them several times, I sat at the base of a big tree in a huff. I couldn't believe we got separated. Then I heard laughter, softly at first. As each family member emerged from behind trees, they laughed harder. We didn't get separated, they purposefully "abandoned" me! The more they laughed, the more pissed I got. "Shut up! Why would you do that to me?" Dad hushed them and said, "You need to always be aware of your surroundings, and you don't just wander around if you get lost." I was furious, "How am I supposed to know that when you never told me?" The edges of his mouth curled into a slight grin as he said, "Now you know." I did not appreciate the lesson at that moment, I can assure you.

Leaving me "alone" in the woods was not the only time Dad used experience to teach instead of just telling us something. One time, we were camping next to a river in Canada when I was about ten. Dad asked, "Why don't you come canoeing with Kevin and me?" They maneuvered us into the middle of the river and, we hadn't gone too far when the canoe tipped over and we ended up in the cold, moving water. I quickly figured out that it was a set-up. Dad and Kevin conspired to dump me into the river to see how I would handle it. Needless to say, I was not happy as I swam to shore, stomped back to our campground, and sat in a snit.

When they made it back to camp, Dad told me, "You never leave your boat if you capsize; you stay with it so people can find you." My mouth dropped open, and I shook my head in bewilderment, "I was close to the shore. There was no reason to stay with the canoe when I could just swim to shore, and you never told me I should stay with the boat." It was déjà vu, "Now you know."

62

Everything John experienced growing up—everything we *all* experienced growing up—had some role in how we turned out. And the amazing thing is, we never know *what* will affect us later in life or how. It could be a tiny event like kicking a rock to school with a friend, or something major like defending the defenseless. You never know what will end up being a life lesson.

John developed an interest in cooking at an early age and was always looking for new things to try. He took it way too far after talking with a friend but, who knows, maybe that one event helped him succeed in the survival portion of his CCT training.

Doug Curry was another of John's good friends and was in the process of earning the rank of Eagle Scout in Boy Scouts. He came home from a wilderness survival weekend and explained to John that he had to eat bugs during the training. Doug regaled him with all kinds of stories, but the bug story piqued John's interest.

A week later, I was in my room when a nutty aroma wafted down the hall, and I had to investigate. John was stirring something in a frying pan as he glanced in my direction. I couldn't tell what it was, but it smelled a bit like burnt popcorn. When I asked what it was, he gave me a wry grin and proudly proclaimed, "Beetles." Ummm, what? He recounted Doug's story about the survival weekend and said, "If he can eat bugs, so can I." To prepare his snack and make it more palatable (if that's even possible), John pulled the wings and legs off a bunch of brown beetles and fried them in butter. That is definitely not how Doug did it, but John was content with his ingenious twist on survival food. He said the beetles tasted like popcorn. I took his word for it.

John had to eat some pretty disgusting things when he went through the survival course years later, and that "food" was most definitely not cooked. Maybe, just maybe, this one moment in time, the seemingly insignificant act of eating beetles, helped him muster the nerve he needed to choke down something even more repulsive than bugs.

Toward the end of each school year, seniors put on a school play; some acted in it and others were the stage crew. In my senior year, our class performed *Westside Story*. I went to the tryouts but couldn't sing in front of everyone, so I left. What a chickenshit! I regret not even trying.

John, on the other hand, was a "joiner." He *loved* being part of whatever was happening and wanted to make the most of his final year. As casting time approached, he didn't commit right away. He was dating a junior, and she was the jealous type. She didn't want him to leave her to be with his classmates. He expressed his indecision with Dad, which he wrote about years later in a letter to the 24. It was titled, "A Message from Dad."

I guess the best time to start is John's graduating years. In this message, you will see how John developed his tenacity to go into a project with the idea to do his very best.

To: Colonel Kenneth Rodriguez and the rest of the 24th Special Tactics Squadron

Starting his senior year in high school, John sat down with me to talk. He said, "Dad, I have a problem, and I don't know what to do about it." He went on to say that tryouts for the senior class play were beginning, and his girlfriend, who was a class behind him, didn't want him to go out for it. My comment was, "Girls will come and go in your life, and your senior year in high school is only once in your life. You must decide if, 1) are you going to let a girl make your decisions for you, and, 2) are you going to let a once-in-a-lifetime year go to waste?" He went with the senior year.

John chose to make memories that would last a lifetime instead of caving to the pressures of someone else. It's a lesson I wish I had learned; the "someone else" that kept me from my play was me.

Their senior class play was *Mame,* and John had multiple small roles. He was happy to be part of the extras on stage, putting in long hours and the hard work of learning his few lines and practicing dance routines with his cast members. Yes, that's right—dance routines! We have proof.

As much fun as he had while practicing and performing, a few little birdies told me he liked the after-parties even more—and not just after the actual performances. The grapevine was abuzz with whispers of cast parties after rehearsals too. It was at those parties that he got to know several people he had only known in passing. Yes, some were females who were giddy over finally getting to spend time with "the nice, cute guy" known as John Chapman. He made the most of his last months of high school with kids he had spent the past twelve years growing up alongside.

For most kids in the play, *Mame* and graduation were the final times they ever spent with John. The memories they have of him are of a happy and caring guy—someone they wanted to hang out with. I heard from many of his classmates after his death, all of them expressing utter disbelief that John Chapman, the kid they knew and partied with, had died in a war in a far-off land. What they did believe, though, is that he gave his life to save others.

It's impossible to know when you're seeing someone for the very last time, so cherish every moment and be kind.

8

Sharing Middle Child

There is no time like the old time,
when you and I were young.
~ Oliver Wendell Holmes, Sr.

I am a year and a half older than John, so I never knew a time without him; he was always there. Mom has a baby photo of him lying in my doll's stroller while I stood at the handle. He was my little plaything for a brief moment in time. As we grew, John and I were close but certainly not without rivalry. Maybe it was because we shared the middle child role or because we were both competitive and loved to one-up each other. Perhaps that's just who we were, but we had our share of brother/ sister battles that sometimes started with or escalated to anger and almost always ended in laughter. I could never stay angry at John. None of us could; he had a special bond with all of us, each one different from the other, but laughter was commonly shared.

When we were in our tween years, John, Tammy, and I found trouble when we decided to jump on our beds. Mom and Dad were out on separate errands, so we jumped until we were sweaty and thirsty. John volunteered to get some water while Tammy and I continued bouncing. As he stood at the kitchen sink, Dad walked in the back door. There's no telling if John saw him pull into the driveway; all I know is Tammy and I were caught, and we weren't going down without him. Mom was at the grocery store, so Dad announced his punishment, "You all have to jump on the living room floor until your mom comes home." We were horrified. Mom always took way longer than she said she would. I was so pissed at John. I was sure he could have done something to warn us that Dad had come home.

Time warps when you are doing physical penance, and questions race through your mind: How long will Mom take today? Why didn't John let us know Dad was home? And why is it so darn hard to jump on the floor? We had been jumping for what felt like hours when John started joking around, and my fury at him grew. He turned it up a notch by dramatically yelling, "Agony! Oh, aaaagony!" I uttered through gritted teeth, "Shut. Up." He kept it up and gradually succeeded in making the three of us laugh. Truthfully, it was the four of us. Dad chuckled at his antics too, which ultimately saved us. He knew Mom could be gone a long time, so he allowed the punishment-turned-comedy to be the end of his creative discipline. We crumbled to the floor; our legs too rubbery to do anything else.

John had a way of making you feel as though you were the most important person to him at that moment in time whether he just met you or had known you for years. But brothers and sisters *have* to have their squabbles, don't they? It must be written somewhere. While John and I usually shared the middle child spot peacefully, we sometimes fought to be #1 Middle Child. The natural competition between us saw victory changing hands, wrenched back and forth like an occasional tug-of-war with a giant mud puddle awaiting the loser. A particularly epic battle happened one summer when we were teens. We were trading verbal barbs, trying to one-up each other. The cause of this battle has long since been lost to the place of insignificant arguments, but I will never forget how it all went down.

The battle of wits began in the kitchen, and I was used to winning this type of skirmish. I was cocksure, reveling every time I sent a zinger straight into him. With each small victory, I tasted blood and pressed on, looking to crush him in our battle of teenage badinage. My verbal advance continued, or was it John's retreat? In my mind, he was retreating. He was staying in the game but had physically moved into the living room, turning to face me in his last stand. I was confident; after all, I usually won the verbal clashes. I advanced to the doorway between the kitchen (the start of the battle) and the living room (what would be my victory ground) and loudly planted my wooden Dr. Scholls® sandals firmly at shoulder width. He launched a volley as he squared off about six feet in front of me. Admittedly, it was a good one, but I was able to muster an immediate counterattack, certain he was going down in flames. Without hesitation, John fired the shot that turned my expected triumph into a crushing defeat. I had nothing. No response. No comeback. I exhaled as fury simmered over my demise.

John stood firm, waiting for something—anything. He had turned confident and cocky. My shock over having no response morphed into a physical reaction as he taunted me with his win. I kicked out my right foot in frustration, not intending it to be anything more than that. When my leg snapped forward, the heavy wooden sandal flew off and headed straight toward John's head. He didn't move, not even a flinch, as the projectile sailed so closely over him that it tousled his light brown hair on the way by. I watched in horror as my sandal missed his head and landed with a *thunk* into the ceiling before plummeting to the floor. Silence filled the room as we gasped and held our collective breath. John looked up then lowered his gaze at me. The corners of his mouth crawled slowly up his cheeks as he looked back up at the small crater, looked back at me with knowing eyes, and let loose a barrage of loud laughter and jeers, "Haha! You're in trouble now! No way you can hide *that*!" I had fallen face down in our tug-o-war mud puddle. And just like that, victory was his.

Once John exhausted his jabs and I accepted defeat, we started to giggle. I laughed with relief that I hadn't nailed him in the middle of the forehead with my wooden missile. The ceiling could be patched—not so sure about his head, even as thick as it was.

Isn't it funny how small things can remind you of something long forgotten? I recently found a box of Precious Moments figurines I thought had been lost in a move. One caught my attention: Faith Takes the Plunge. The little girl is marching forward, a scowl on her face and a toilet plunger in her hand. There was a note in the box, "As soon as I saw this, I thought of you. I hope you like it. Love, Tammy." I laughed out loud as I remembered why she gave it to me so many years ago. Two family members were known for regularly needing that particular bathroom accessory; I was one. Tammy's comical "jab" also reminded me of when I had trouble one day. Dad and John were in the living room when I came out of the bathroom, plunger in hand. John started teasing me about needing it … again. I squared off in front of him and said, "Shut up or I'll plunge your face!" Dad almost fell out of his chair laughing and John's jaw dropped open before he followed up with his cackle. I was not amused then. It's hysterical to me now. I love that this forgotten memory was brought back by Tammy's gift.

As you may have figured out by now, John liked to test all of us, and he enjoyed our back-and-forth banter as much as I did. As far as he was concerned, it was just good-natured fun, but sometimes he pressed his luck with some antic or another and paid the price, especially when we were teenagers. He chose the wrong audience one afternoon—Mom. Thinking he was so clever, he actually tried to get away with swearing in front of her. He grinned and said, "Fother Mucker," but she wasn't fooled or amused. His reward for the crafty curse was having a bar of Dial® soap wiped on his tongue and, let me tell you, that is *not* pleasant; or so I've heard.

Usually, John targeted one of us kids for his silliness, not Mom or Dad. One evening, I became his intended victim. We were lying on the couch, his head on one armrest and mine on the other, our bodies overlapping in the middle. His legs were longer, so he stuck his foot in my face. I knocked it away and told him to stop, but, wonder of wonders, he kept doing it until I finally said, "If you stick your foot in my face one more time, I'm going to bite your big toe." He thought about it for a nano-second, then slowly and purposefully maneuvered his foot in my face, holding it millimeters from my mouth, daring me to follow through with my threat. Using just my teeth (I didn't want his nasty toe in my mouth), I bit down hard and only long enough to make my point. He yanked away, grabbed his foot, and yelled, "I can't believe you actually bit my toe!" He didn't stick his foot in my face again—at least not that night.

He chose a different body part another time. I sat at the end of our kitchen table, a toothpick clenched in my teeth, as John baked who knows what. Every time he checked the oven, he stepped back much farther than he needed to so his butt would be in my face. I didn't let it go on for long, "Stop or I'll stick you with my toothpick." Always pushing the envelope, he stepped back once more, making sure his rear end was as close as he could get it without touching my face. He couldn't help himself! Maybe he didn't think I'd actually follow through with my threat, but he was painfully wrong. In one swift move, I plucked the toothpick from my mouth and stuck him with it as hard as I dared. He howled, rubbed his wounded cheek, and immediately launched into his "this is really funny" cackle, and I was thoroughly satisfied.

We definitely had our moments, but it wasn't all banter and fights. Most of our childhood was silly and fun and sometimes compassionate. One time, when I was seventeen and John was sixteen, we were in the kitchen (it seems like a lot of our interactions were in the kitchen). I was getting breakfast before school, and we were talking about nothing in particular when he stopped and looked at me. I got defensive, "Why are you looking at me?" I steeled myself for the jab he would surely throw my way. His demeanor changed almost imperceptibly as he considered how to convey his thoughts. His expression was soft as he said, "You know, you might want to change how you apply your eye shadow. You did a good job, but you have to put it all the way …" and he showed me what he meant. He noticed how most of the girls were wearing makeup and didn't want me to be the odd one. His comment could easily have turned into an argument, but I knew he didn't mean it as a dig; he was only trying to help me.

Maybe John and I got along so well because we both had a bit of smart ass in us. (Say it isn't so.) Even a normal situation could become something more when one of us would do something unexpected to ramp it up, like one summer afternoon when we were in our mid-teens. I was cutting a juicy orange at the kitchen table when John walked in the back door and stopped. Shirtless from doing yardwork, his blue eyes lit up when he saw me cutting the orange. Sweat trickled from his tousled brown hair as he asked if I would throw him half of my snack. Without hesitating, I picked up the cut orange and threw it overhand at him. He was usually very good at catching, or at least dodging, unexpected projectiles, but this time there was no time to react. The orange half

73

rocketed through the air and landed with a *splat* right in the middle of his chest and stuck there. John looked down at the orange suctioned to his chest like a remora to a shark then raised his gaze to my shocked face. We burst into the kind of belly laughs that hurt so good.

It would not be the last time I threw food at John as though I was trying to get the runner out at first. One year, I hosted Thanksgiving when John was home on leave. He sat opposite me at the table, and, as we settled in for dinner, he asked, "Hey Lori, throw me a roll, will you?" Smart-ass me picked up a roll and pitched it overhand at him. His reflexes were lightning fast as he lifted his hand and caught the roll, curling his fingers around it as he gave me a knowing grin. There were a couple of disapproving scowls but—my house, my rules. John cackled and that was all the approval I needed. I dearly miss his cackle.

After we were all grown and out of the house, our time with John was mostly reduced to phone calls or what was known as IMs, instant (typed) messages, that happened over the Internet in real-time. It was quite innovative! In-person visits with him were few and far between, which made it extra special when we could arrange it. In my mid-twenties, Kevin talked me into taking karate lessons with him. I knew nothing about martial arts but figured, "Why not?" Kyokushin[1], which means "the ultimate

---

[1] After one to two years, the schools in Connecticut changed the name to USA Oyama but testing for black belt still happened in New York City at the Kyokushin School. I don't claim to understand the name change, though it may have had something to do with the original school in Japan.

truth," originated in Japan and is full-contact karate founded by a Korean-Japanese named Masutatsu (Mas) Oyama.[2] I *loved* it. There were no "time served/money paid" promotions; if you didn't earn it, you didn't get to test, no matter how long you took classes. We learned traditional Kyokushin punches, kicks, and stances as well as forms called *katas*, but we were also taught self-defense and street fighting. My self-confidence grew enough that I continued taking classes even when Kevin stopped.

John came home on leave and was eager to watch me test for one of the higher belts. I was so excited to show him my skills, especially since he had been taught martial arts as a Combat Controller. Once testing started, the last thing on my mind was the audience. The tests were no joke, let me tell you. We had to spar with higher belts, perform self-defense techniques, do progressively harder katas, and when we lined up at the end of testing, our *sensei* whacked each of us multiple times with a *shinai*—a Japanese sword, usually bamboo, used for training. The shinai hits tested how well one could take blows and not flinch. Though our sensei did not execute full-power contact, it still stung. While our sensei and *sempais*[3] conferred about our performances, I snuck a glance in John's direction. We were supposed to look straight ahead,

---

[2] Heaney, Scott. "The Beginner's Guide to Kyokushin Karate." The Martial Way. March 18, 2016. https://the-martial-way.com/the-beginners-guide-to-kyokushin-karate/

[3] Both sensei and sempai are black belts of varying degrees, but in Kyokushin, sensei is the highest-ranking black belt and/or owner of the school.

but I couldn't help it. He was leaning back in his chair, legs outstretched and arms crossed over his chest, and he was smiling. He nodded ever so slightly, and I savored his pride in me. Once I received my new rank and testing was declared over, John rewarded me with one of his signature bear hugs and whispered, "Damn! Remind me not to mess with you. Congratulations." His admiration meant as much to me as earning my belt. I was elated that John had been able to attend my grueling test. It was the only time he saw me kick some karate butt.

Though John couldn't make it home very often, he made sure to let us know we were in his thoughts. Back in the "olden days," when everyone had an answering machine, I saved any message he left, at least for a short time. Unfortunately, after he died, I only had one message, "Hey Lori, guess what? I love you." It was short and very sweet; I still have it. He found silly ways to let me know he was thinking of me. "Hello? I'd like to order a pepperoni pizza." And he always ended with, "I love you." I will never forget how those messages from John made me feel. It took him only seconds, but it made my entire day, and if I saved them, those messages made my day after day.

Often, when he was away on TDY (temporary duty), we found ourselves the only ones on the old-fashioned IMs, and I coveted those times. I had him all to myself as we chatted about anything and everything. If I asked where he was, he'd just say, "Yeaaahhh." Mostly, we talked about ourselves, family, and dreams. My dream at that point was to not be alone. I worked two jobs, had Rachel, owned a house, and hated going to clubs, so meeting men was relegated to the workplace. It is not a good idea. I do *not* recommend it. John would always comfort me, "Don't worry, I'll find someone for you." I didn't know how that was possible with me in Connecticut and him in North Carolina, but I liked that he said he'd try. Years later, he found a way.

I treasure my memories of growing up with John—with all of my siblings. When we fought, we fought hard. When we played, we played hard. John was sometimes like an annoying fly that kept buzzing by my ear but, in the end, he could usually make me admit I rather liked the fly.

9

Young Adulthood—Compassion, Mischief, and, of course, Alcohol

You only get one life. It is actually your duty to live it as fully as possible.
~ Jojo Moyes Author of *Me Before You*

By the time John entered high school, he had established himself as one who drew others to him by being true to who he was. He never took himself very seriously; instead, he sought fun and took calculated risks. He pulled special people into his orbit, choosing to cultivate close and lasting friendships with a select few. Some were drawn in only briefly, but the time they *did* have with John left lasting impressions.

One of those "a moment in time" people is Kelly (Cray) Savery. When John died, there were two ceremonies in Windsor Locks: a street renamed for him, and the unveiling of a memorial at the high school. After the high school ceremony, Kelly revealed her story—one that would not surprise those who knew him. She will never forget the day John touched her life in high school. She shared her story again in a letter to me.

My father had passed away in September of my freshman year. I remember returning to school on a Monday after taking the two weeks allowed for a death in the family. I had taken a deep breath at the door, steeling myself to do this. Before I even reached my locker, at least half a dozen kids approached me to express their condolences—small-town people always know these things—and it felt like everything was moving in slow motion.

I vaguely remember hearing the bell ring and found myself wandering down a hallway near the back entrance of the building. Then I was outside. I sat on a cement light-post base, and my head was swimming. I was not ready for this.

I don't know for sure how long I sat there, but all of a sudden, someone was walking up behind me, and I heard a voice asking if I was ok. I was crying and not really wanting to talk to anybody. Somehow, though, this boy who I didn't really know well—I knew who he was but never hung out with him because he was a year older—somehow knew what to do. He just sat next to me and didn't say a word. He put a hand on my arm and just let me cry.

At some point, he said, "I'm John. What can I do to help?" I told him I just wasn't ready to deal with school, and I was thinking about going home. He asked where I lived, and when I told him it was across town, he said he would walk me home if

I wanted him to. We talked a bit, and I told him I didn't want him to get into trouble for leaving school. I think he laughed at me! I finally agreed to go back in with him and go to the nurse's office. He walked with me and waited until someone was there to talk to me. He gave me a hug and said he hoped I felt better soon.

I will never forget the kindness shown by this young man, actually still a boy, to a stranger that he saw in pain and couldn't just walk away from.

I was later fortunate enough to work with him over the summer at the park where he was a lifeguard at the pool, and I worked in the recreation building. He was charming, funny, smart, cute, and everyone's friend; that was John Chapman. He was someone who made an impression on me and affected my life in a way I don't think he ever realized. I will never forget him.

In June 2020, forty-one years after Kelly's heartfelt encounter with John, she reached out to me with a little reminder of just how much John affected her life.

Hey Lori! I just wanted to tell you that I had a chance to go for a walk with my twelve-year-old grandson over the weekend. I often go down "John's Street" off of Southwest Avenue to visit the flag and memorial plaque. I told Alex about John and your family, and my sweet boy said, "Wow, so he was a hero, right? I'll add them to my prayers." I just wanted you to know that he will not be forgotten, even by people he never met.

My dear Kelly, kind messages like yours bring joy to my heart and help ease the pain that always lingers, sometimes dulled and beneath the surface, sometimes raw and right on top. Thank you.

Suzy (Lindberg) Binegar was another young girl who was a bit enamored with John long ago. She met him at Hopmeadow Country Club in Simsbury, Connecticut, when he was a lifeguard and diving coach. It was his senior year, and Suzy was a wide-eyed 15-year-old who was a little surprised John would take the time to be friendly with someone "so much younger." When I spoke with her, she was happy to talk about their friendship; to share the John she knew.

> Aside from being adorable, John was a ton of fun and treated us really well. He was one of the only lifeguards who would let us get away with a lot. John was a lot of fun; he was full of life. He was just a kind spirit—and I was smitten, but he was 18 and I was 15 and he was very patient with all of us girls that summer. We worked on our tans just so we could be there on the days he was working. He was adorable, but also funny and confident in himself; he just had a presence where he knew who he was and where he was going.

We started a nice little friendship, and he went to college the following year, he but kept in touch via letters over the years. We lost touch when I went off to college and reconnected my senior year. One of the last letters I remember having shortly before my graduation was him telling me how proud he was of me and I was so blown away. I was proud of *him* and the service he was doing for us.

After that, I hadn't seen him for probably five or six years when we met at *One Way Fair* in Simsbury, which was the old train station. We had a burger and a beer and just caught up. It was sweet—old friends getting together and reconnecting. It was nice to … it's funny, in life, you meet somebody and then you can go a long time without chatting and you get the unexpected letter. To be able to get together and pick up conversation and, before you know it, three hours have passed. We each had someplace to be, so we said our goodbyes and off we went.

That's just kind of how it was; the occasional letters and cards through college and keeping apprised of each other's life. It was interesting, he had sent me one of his pictures when he was in uniform, and I kept the card. It was in a box of correspondence and things I kept over the years from many people. My husband and I had a flood in the basement, and we lost everything that was down there. We went through everything; I was trying to go through things and kind of keep track of what was going to be thrown out. If there was anything of importance in a box, I had to write it down and I knew we were losing a lot of pictures. It was the strangest thing: I moved this pile of things aside and the one thing that fell out was his picture, so I was able to save it. Out of that whole wad of papers, of everything that was soaking wet, this one little picture flittered out and it was kind of neat. The only other thing that fell out of another pile was one of the first letters I got from my husband when we were dating.

When I heard about John—I remember the day—I was getting ready for work, turned on the news, and there was his face. I was gobsmacked; I couldn't believe it.

Suzy paused a moment, remembering it all … her time with him, his friendship, and the shock of finding out that he had been killed in a far-off land, defending our country. She was proud of him … and very sad. It must have been surreal, as it was for so many: Hey, I knew him. He was my friend. And now he's gone. I asked her if there was anything else she remembered about John.

It was just the spirit of him … he *made* you want to keep in touch, and it could have been every six months, every year, or a couple of years would go by. It was a simpler time [when we first met]. I mean, 18 seemed like a massive age spread back then, so for him to take time and be kind to us girls, and not dismiss the annoying teenage girls … And he was so talented. We challenged him to dive-offs and he would double-bounce so he could get more height. It was a nice time in my life. And then to keep in touch through college, and then when he went into the service. He was the first person I knew in my generation who had gone off to serve. It left a mark. The more I read and the more I researched and learned about what a hero he was in so many ways … what a sacrifice. But, as tragic as it is, I don't think he would have done it any different. That was, that was just him … service first, others first, and that's quite remarkable in this day and age where we're such an immediate gratification, self-serving generation. Every now and then, you take a moment and be grateful. Not a lot of people leave a mark like he did. There are lots of folks with us every day that don't leave that kind of mark.

We never knew how many lives John impacted until after he sacrificed his. I am convinced there are many more stories that we have yet to hear. If you, dear reader, have one of those lost stories, I'm all ears and sitting on the edge of my lawn chair by our imaginary bonfire. Come share your story.

Meanwhile, I have to say that John was no saint; Lord knows he did plenty to kill that idea. I'm sure some people didn't like him, but as a non-objective and biased sister, I think those who didn't like him were just jealous, or maybe he was a smartass one too many times. He had this incredible ability to fit in wherever he found himself, and he accepted everyone without judgment. He also knew when to step up and do the right thing even if no one was watching. I should say *especially* when no one was there as witness; he never needed hard slaps on the back in sports, and he certainly did not care about recognition for being a good Samaritan.

John was far ahead of his time. In the 1980s, kids were not taught that *everyone* is special and deserves respect, and many children with disabilities were shunned and, at times, the targets of some pretty brutal bullying. Lynn (Noyes) Klein was a cherished friend of John's during high school. She remembered a classmate who had to endure relentless teasing because of the challenges she faced. It wasn't cool to be seen with her and it was definitely not advisable to defend her. Lynn was in awe of how John was friendly to their classmate when no one else was, and he didn't care who saw. She recalled,

> Whenever he was talking with her, and just being her friend, and the way that he didn't care who was watching. That was just so. . . not something you did back then. He would sit and talk with her on the curb, not caring who saw them, and that's the way John was with her; he was just so . . . out of a different time in the way that he could be the kid who's out on the soccer field and roughing it up, and yet he had the most gentle heart of anybody.

John did have a gentle heart for many people, but not for bullies. In his senior year, he learned about someone in his class who regularly picked on underclassmen. That raised John's hackles, so he pulled the guy aside and told him, in no uncertain terms, that he would not touch those kids again. The response to his declaration was a challenge, "Oh yeah? Meet me out back after school and we'll see about that." John knew he was placing himself in the crosshairs of this kid who was much bigger; he didn't care. John was going to fight for the younger ones. After the school day ended, he headed for the designated site to find the other kid already there, waiting to pummel him; a crowd of onlookers had assembled to witness the presumed bloodbath. As he approached, the kid raised his hands in a fighting stance, expecting John to do the same. Instead, John squared off in front of his challenger and dropped him to the ground with a roundhouse kick to the head. The crowd fell silent as jaws dropped to the ground. Satisfied, John turned and quietly walked away. The battle was over before it began, and the bullying stopped because John had the courage to stand up to the "mean boy" even though the kid probably could have beaten the crap out of him under the right circumstances.

As we reached our mid-teens, Dad told each of us, "I was your age once. I know you're going to try things. I just want you to know that I might not say anything, but if your mother ever catches you, I'm backing her. Just be safe." I think Kevin and John took advantage of that implied permission more than Tammy and I did. John was a calculated risk-taker. He would consider the worst-case outcome and then decide whether it was worth the risk like he did when he escaped being sent to his room. Whatever he contemplated usually ended up being worth the risk, and it drove me nuts. I swear that kid could get away with anything, like when he played hooky. Every September, Springfield, Massachusetts, hosts a huge event called The Eastern States Exposition, otherwise known as The Big E. The grounds are enormous, and they have everything from amusement rides and games to food trucks and permanent buildings representing each New England state. Hundreds of vendors line the streets. There are horse shows and livestock exhibitions. Everyone looked forward to the Big E.

I listened as friends chattered about their exploits at the fair, which was only twelve miles from town. Some of them skipped school to go, but I never dared for fear of being caught. Plus, I *liked* school. (I know; don't say it.) One year—it had to be my senior year and John's junior year—he pulled a disappearing act at school and resurfaced at the Big E. I don't know who his co-conspirators were (I could guess) or who drove, but there's no doubt he had several buddies with him when they absconded across the state line. He told me afterward, and I could not believe it. Once again, I was jealous *and* impressed; he had the nerve to risk getting caught in favor of an afternoon of fun. Let me be clear, the risk wasn't necessarily that the school would find out; it was if *Mom* found out. John figured the worst-case scenario would be grounding, and he was fine with that.

Many, many times over the years I have wished I could be as carefree as he was.

Where are my manners? How are you doing so far, my dear reader? I would offer you some of Dad's famous chili if I could. I may not be able to supply creature comforts for you, but I pray our "fireside chat" is entertaining. Now where was I? Ah, yes! Mischief!

The "bike-in-the-tree" caper years prior wasn't the only one to go awry for John. Barely teenagers, he and Tammy hid inside our thick, four-foot-high hedges, spying on kids across the street. Most were older teens, but one was John's age. The fence in front of the house kitty-corner from ours was a favorite pot-smoking hangout, so John decided to scare them into going home. He thought if he threw something in their direction, they would leave. He crawled around until he discovered a broken piece of our crumbling asphalt driveway; it was the best projectile he could find. With the intent of it landing just near enough to scare them, John let it fly as he and Tammy ducked behind the hedges, giggling softly at his brilliance. Instead of landing at their feet, John's warning shot hit the younger kid on the top of his head. He had been straddling his bike when—*wham!* He never saw it coming.

John's giggles evaporated when he peeked over the hedge to see their reaction. Satisfaction morphed into horror as he realized the projectile missed the mark and had, instead, crashed hard onto the boy's head; blood was already inching down his forehead. While the older kids stood around discussing what to do, John rose from cover, put the kid on the handlebars, and rode him home to his parents. He walked home dejected and unhappy with how his "brilliant" plan had failed and embarrassed that the kids now knew what he had done.

As with Tammy's story, our hedges often gave us a false sense of invisibility and courage. When John and I were in our mid-teens, we were home alone one wintery evening and boredom nagged at us. That's never a good thing! Dusk was creeping in as we went outside to toss snowballs at passing cars. We ducked behind the hedges so they wouldn't know who threw them. Newly fallen snow left the roads slick and slippery; we were oblivious. Only a few moving targets drove slowly by, and the last one made us regret not staying inside. As it crept along the road, John lobbed a baseball-sized snowball that hit—*splat!*—squarely on the driver's side of the windshield. We were too slow; the guy saw us as we ducked and huddled together, laughing because there was no way he could get to us inside our yard. In a shocking twist, prey became hunter as he threw his car into park, got out, and tried to chase us. The hedges were too thick for him to push through, so we took off for the back of the house, tumbling through the back door on top of each other. John locked it, and we melted into the floor, praying for invisibility should he peek in the window. Our angry pursuer ran around the hedges and sprinted to the front door, ringing the doorbell insistently several times. He eventually gave up and left. As we breathed giant sighs of relief, the adrenaline escaped our bodies in the form of laughter. We weren't laughing at the man; it was nervous laughter over getting away. No cackling came from John that time.

There was no "making it right" in that instance. We were convinced the man would have killed us and were actually very surprised he never returned to speak with Mom and Dad. I will neither confirm nor deny whether similar wintery mischief ever happened again from within the hedges on Andover Road.

When we were growing up—ancient times according to my son—the drinking age was eighteen, and it was usually easy (but not always) for underage kids to score ill-begotten spirits. Aside from sports, school, and church, there wasn't much to do in town, so John and his buddies jumped at the challenge to acquire whatever rotgut they could find, which they then took to some clandestine location, like the woods near St. Robert's church. It was common practice with those guys.

One summer afternoon, I was home with Mom when John and his friend Chris Daniel sauntered in the back door. Mom was doing chores, so she kept popping in and out of the living room; it's a good thing she did not settle in to visit. I rose from the couch when John left to get something from his bedroom. Chris swayed in the middle of the living room, so I stood in front of him in case he lost his balance. I choked on laughter as Mom made small talk with him, never realizing that he was wasted. When John emerged, he passed Mom, and his telltale glossy eyes screamed, "I'm drunk!" I escorted them to the back door, and John put a wavering finger up to his lips and grinned—his brilliant blue eyes filled with mischief. I know it was irresponsible to let them go (they were not driving), but things were different back then, and we were kids. It also wouldn't be the last time I ran interference for my inebriated younger brother.

Skeet Tersavich had a graduation party and unattended alcohol tantalized fifteen-year-old John from the picnic table. Sly as he was, he bided his time until partygoers were chased inside by darkness and the backyard was vacant. He kept disappearing out the back door, and not one of us noticed. When he came to me in the kitchen, I was shocked to find him barely able to stand. He cackled about his stealthy booze consumption and teetered near the wall. There was no way he could pull off looking sober. I ordered him to stay put while I did some recon. If anyone headed toward the kitchen, I raced back to drag John around the corner. It seemed an eternity—like we did the "hide John" shuffle all night—but it was only a half hour or so. I slapped my hand on his chest and held him against the wall to keep him standing. When I had to let go, he slithered down the wall, slumping into a heap just as Mom said we were heading home. My only chance to keep John "safe" was getting him to the van before anyone else. No matter how much I begged Dad, "Let me drive home," he would not give me the keys, so I quickly came up with Plan B. I wrapped my arm around John's waist and draped his arm over my shoulders. Through clenched teeth, I told him not to speak, and I joined his goofy (drunk) act as we made our way to the van; he was always clowning around, so it fit my plan perfectly. Man, I was slick! I slid the side door open, shoved him in, and he crawled into one of the seats, slumping to one side. *That* was not going to work. I lowered the bench seat in the back into a bed and somehow flopped him onto it. Then, with every turn Dad took, John rolled to that side of the van, dramatically flailing his arms as he did. And with every melodramatic rolling to the side, I was growing more and more pissed. Shockingly, I got him into the house without Mom or Dad noticing his condition; I let them go in first. By that time, my patience and humor about the situation had completely vaporized, so I unceremoniously dropped him off at his room; he was no longer my concern. Much to my satisfaction, John was a "hurting unit" most of the next day. Years later, Dad disclosed that he knew the whole time and that's why he wouldn't give me the keys. "Now you know."

John drank alone that night, but he usually had at least one co-conspirator. Billy Brooks, the new boy in kindergarten who John saved from certain annihilation, shared his first time drinking hard liquor. Guess who was involved? John wanted him to go to a party, but Billy balked, confessing, "Aside from a beer or two, I never drank much before." John dismissed Billy's reluctance, saying, "Oh, come on, come on. We're gonna go." Once he relented, John asked, "Well, what do you want?" Billy was confused, "What do you mean, 'What do I want?'" John's eyes sparkled with mischief and he said, "I'll get you a bottle." His mind raced in search of a quick answer and all he could say was, "Yukon Jack." John chuckled but procured the liquor, and Billy managed to down most of the bottle that night. The party had been a blast; the next morning not so much.

I have no doubt there are countless more tales of John and his friends finding the liquid courage needed for some of their high jinks, but many of those stories remain secreted in their memories. If any of his cohorts wish to share now, I do believe the statute of limitations has long since expired.

10

Sports—Soccer and Diving

To build a strong team, you must see someone else's strength as a complement to your weakness and not a threat to your position or authority.
~ Christine Caine

When Dad was growing up in the 1950s in central Michigan, soccer didn't exist, at least not in his world. Football was *the* sport so, besides running track and playing baseball, Dad's focus was on football. He played until he broke his collarbone during his senior year of high school.

In 1970, Kevin was almost nine and wanted to join the town soccer league. As Dad and Kevin waited for team assignments, Dad was surprised when they included coaches. He suddenly found himself the coach of a sport he knew nothing about. He had no choice but to step up, learn the game, and become a good coach to those boys. His plan of attack was simple: Read books about soccer and, more importantly, go to high school games and practices; go to college games; pay close attention to how the game was played *and* how it was coached.

During his field trips, he brought Kevin so he could see soccer in action too. John tagged along on most of their scouting missions and was a sideline observer for their own practices and games. He grew tired of only being able to watch, so at six years old, he asked Dad if he could join the team. Since there were no teams for kids that young, John became Kevin's teammate, and his love and mastery of the game began.

Coaching was trial and error for Dad, and he knew soccer was new to his little players too. Watching games had helped him understand it better, so he often had his team meet him at high school matches. He took what he liked from the coaching style of Dan Sullivan, the Windsor Locks High coach, and ignored what he didn't. He became a student of the game, which became apparent when his little team started winning. Even though John was a couple of years younger than his teammates, he became an integral part of those early boys' teams. He understood the game right away and learned ball control skills to the point that Dad used him to demonstrate for other players. In later years when Dad coached the town girls' team, and to the delight of many, John once again helped train the players. He was able to teach without making his "students" feel inferior, and if someone had difficulty performing a particular skill, he took the time to figure out a different way of explaining it. John was patient and fun and funny with everyone under his tutelage; he was the best assistant Dad could have had.

Prior to the formation of girls' teams decades ago, any girl who wanted to play soccer had to play on the boys' teams, so that's what I did. I played alongside my brothers, learning from them, and John was proud that I was part of his team. As we grew older and I played on girls' teams, there were still times when Dad asked me to bring my gear to a boys' game in case he needed a sub. To their credit, not one boy resented having a girl play with them; they treated me like a sister and protected me like one too. When I was sixteen and John was fifteen, the boys were going to play a team from Mansfield, Connecticut, in Mansfield. Most of their boys played for Mansfield's high school—E.O. Smith—during the school year, and one was the Smith star. They would be a tough team to beat, and it was a sweltering summer day.

Before any away game, Dad drove his van to meet players at the soccer field to see how many were going and who needed a ride. The van could seat six kids comfortably (and legally) in the back, but sometimes, all or most of the team sat waiting for him. Kids sat wherever they could find a spot on the floor. It was as illegal then as it is today. Dad would say, "If we have an accident, anyone who can move needs to walk, crawl, or roll away because we have too many people in here." That day, Dad ended up with extra passengers, including me. He already knew there would only be eleven players for the game, which meant no subs on one of the most humid and oppressive days of the summer. John asked, "Is Lori going to play?" Dad sighed, "If they let her." He asked me to go prepared to play but not suited up; he still had to ask the other coach if I could be a sub. We talked smack about the other team during the forty-five-minute drive to Mansfield. It would be a brutal game, but we were full of bravado when Dad pulled up to the field. As

John jumped from the side door of the van, he turned to me and whispered, "They better let you play!" He jogged onto the field to begin warming up but kept an eye on Dad as he talked with the Mansfield coach.

I was a tiny thing, standing barely a hair over five feet tall. Dad told me to stay on the sideline while he spoke with the other coach, and I watched them with fingers crossed. I *loved* playing soccer. Dad had his back to me, but he turned around, pointed in my direction, then turned back to face the coach. I saw the coach lean past Dad, look at me, and smirk before giving his answer. Their meeting lasted no more than a few minutes. As he came back, I could see the shit-eating grin on Dad's face and the twinkle in his eye. "When I asked if I could use you as a sub since it's such a hot day, he looked over at you and snorted. He said, 'Her? Sure, why not.' and he laughed. Get suited up." John grinned when he saw me emerge from the van with my gear on. He knew that, even though I was only a sub, it meant I'd be on the field a lot to give different guys a break.

It didn't take long for us to figure out that the other team didn't much like playing against a girl. One in particular, the Smith star, decided that if I was going to play with the boys, I was going to be treated like the boys. I never asked for special treatment—bring it! His intent *wasn't* to treat me like one of the boys, though. He was going to teach me a lesson. Mr. Wonderful stood a foot taller than me and was big; he made it his mission to take me out. I played fullback, and John was a midfielder, so he made sure he was close enough to help if I needed it. I held my own, shocking the other team. Big macho Smith kept going after me instead of the ball, and it did not sit well with John or the rest of the team. On one of the last plays before halftime, I found myself chasing the ball; it was halfway between Macho Smith and me. Reaching the ball at the same time, we hit it simultaneously. The ball went nowhere, but Macho Smith's momentum sent him tumbling over the ball. I quickly passed forward and John let loose his "this is funnier than shit" cackle as I ran back to my position, stepping around Not-So-Macho-Now on the way. Beating him felt really good, and I imagine Coach Smirk began to wish he hadn't given Dad permission to use me as a sub.

During halftime, John and a handful of teammates walked over to Big Smith and a couple of other Mansfield players. When the entourage returned to the sideline, Danny Squires laughed as he told me, "We were all getting sick of watching that asshole trying to take you out, so we told him to stay away from you or *we'd* take care of *him*." He didn't go near me during the second half. We didn't win, but our spirits were high. The Windsor Locks boys were something special, especially my little brother who not only accepted me playing on his team but *wanted* me to play.

Over the years, John became a preeminent player, whether for Dad on town teams or for Coach Sullivan at the Windsor Locks High School. Dad called him a general on the field because he had great ball control and the ability to strategize and anticipate where he needed to be on the field at any given moment. He could see where the ball would most likely end up and pre-positioned himself or his teammates where he thought they should be, and he was almost always right.

Though John played for Coach Sullivan all four years of high school, he had an oft-times tumultuous relationship with him. Coach gave him mixed signals—occasionally praising John's talent but more often chastising him for plays that went awry. Many times, those poor plays or missed opportunities were not John's fault, but that of other players, yet Coach still screeched at John. He handled it on the field but showed his frustration at home. Mom remembers well how much Coach Sullivan's treatment bewildered and hurt John. "He would come home, he had played an awesome game, but Coach was on his case all of the time. He'd lay on the couch and say, 'I don't understand it, Mom.' He'd be so upset, almost to the point of tears. I'd tell him, 'You played a good game, and I can't understand why you get yelled at for someone else's mistakes.' That was the biggest struggle he had. I can remember one game in particular; I think it was in West Hartford, and it was a really tough, close game. Coach kept pulling him out, screaming at him, and belittling him in front of *everybody*. Johnny was so upset; he came over to me just before halftime and said, 'Mom, I'm so pissed. I really want to kick the ball in our goal, but I can't do that to my guys.' That's the *only* reason he didn't do it. If it had been between just him and Coach, he would have done it without hesitation. The most heartbreaking thing about it is that from the time he, Brian [Topor], David [Wrabel], and Michael [Toce] were little and first learning the game, when they'd go watch the high school games, they idolized Coach. They all said, 'When we're seniors, we're going to be captains together.' That never happened."

Let's be honest, John was a smartass and perhaps that was part of the issue for Sullivan. He used comedic interludes to diffuse heated tempers or physically draining drills—like jumping on the floor in the living room— and he was gaining a following among his peers because he could laugh things off and make it bearable. At that time, coaches had free reign to teach their charges in whatever manner they wished with little or no pushback from parents. Sullivan's approach was head-on, gruff, and strict, and his coaching methodology was intimidation and belittlement. The problem was, he didn't deploy his methods equally to all of his players. Even players who screwed up on a regular basis enjoyed respite from Coach's tirades. When John realized the inconsistencies, his coping mechanism on the field was humor. He gave 100% for his team, especially in games, but was also quick with comments or physical antics. When giving the eulogy at John's funeral, David Wrabel fondly remembered, "He was not only a peer but often was coaching us at the same time. One of his best qualities, though, was his sense of humor; John was able to bring a smile to most, even when Coach was coming down on us. In fact, John's humor allowed us to receive additional conditioning on the soccer field."

John didn't like Sullivan's coaching style. It was old-school; everyone in town accepted it because he had been a successful coach for so long, but it clashed with John's personality. Beneath his humor and stoicism was a sensitive person who never cared for Sullivan or his approach to coaching. He *wanted* to like Coach but could never figure out how to jump that hurdle. John didn't need constant slaps on the back and loud accolades; that wasn't the issue. The issue was him getting blamed for things he didn't do, and there was rarely an "atta-boy" to soften the sting of the barrage of unwarranted criticism. During John's junior year, Coach had hip surgery and couldn't fulfill his coaching commitment. His temporary replacement was Mark Nolan, a talented young graduate from the University of Hartford who had also played for Sullivan at Windsor Locks High. When Sullivan returned, he was on crutches and couldn't be as active as he usually was, so he used John on many occasions as his on-field assistant—a HUGE mixed signal.

The inconsistency of Coach's treatment of John bewildered all of us. He occasionally watched John dive when it was swim season and remarked about how good he was calling him "a superb athlete." Then soccer season came and there were no compliments, just ridicule and blame. It couldn't be just Coach's style because he didn't spread the criticism to all of his players. Some boys never got called out, so the argument of "coaching style" doesn't cut it. He would intimidate and embarrass the boys if nothing else worked, but usually only targeted a certain few.

One day, our girls' team had a home game, and the boys were practicing nearby. They either had a bad game the previous day or they weren't performing well during practice, so the next thing we knew, the entire boys' team was standing on our sideline. We looked at each other like, "Well, *that's* new." On the way home, John explained our unexpected sideline guests. "Coach was so pissed at us, he turned red. He said, 'You guys can't play like you know what you're doing? Fine. We're going to watch the girls' game so you can learn how to play soccer. I want you to watch Lori Chapman most of all. *She* knows how to play.'" I was mortified! How would any boy on the team like me if Coach called me out like that (I had a crush on pretty much all of them)? More than that, though, I was pissed for John because I thought Coach figured he would be the most embarrassed since his sister was the one singled out. Epic failure. John was proud of me and happy that it *was* me who Coach used as an example.

Remembering that story brings me pride, not in myself, but in John. He always shared the spotlight, shared credit, or even stepped back to let someone else shine. He didn't need constant reassurance and validation. John had more assists on the soccer field than goals, and it's because he didn't need to be the one to score; he just wanted the team to win, and if that meant giving the score to someone else, he did it. And he was very good at it.

In July 2020, I received an email from Jimmy Grandahl. I went to school with his sister Diane and played soccer with her and another sister Barb (*she* was tough!). Jimmy's words brought me to tears.

Thank you for sharing Johnny's story; I cannot imagine how difficult it was to write [*Alone at Dawn*]. I wanted to share my story of Johnny and how he impacted me as a young man.

My family is a soccer family and was no doubt influenced by growing up with your family. Some of my fondest childhood memories were spending weekends on the sidelines of Coach Gene and Coordinator Terry's squad at some tournament. That team was like the WNT [Women's National Team] to me . . . you, Barb, Morf [Maureen Walsh], Tammy, and the rest of the girls helped develop my love for the game.

Despite being around your family for years, I didn't really get a chance to spend time with Johnny until I entered high school. My freshman year was his senior year. I was a boy and he and the rest of the seniors were men. That core crew were like demigods to us young players. We had grown up watching Johnny, [Brian] Topor, Mike Toce, and the rest of the guys battle on that hard dusty pitch. They seemed so fast and so strong.

As you probably remember, the '80s were a bit different than today. That meant ritualized forms of initiation and "hazing"—nothing terrible, but frightening and a bit painful nonetheless. Before one especially terrifying drill, wherein all freshmen stood in the goal with their eyes closed while the upperclassmen shot from the eighteen [yard line], I can remember Johnny pulling me aside and telling me the following: "Jimmy, you are a good player. This is not about trying to hurt you, it is about seeing if you can overcome the fear. If you do, these guys will respect you, as they know you will do anything for them on the field. It is about becoming part of the brotherhood."

I am sure that is not 100% verbatim, but it is how I remember the conversation and the message that resonated with me. All week long—hell week—he would give little looks here and there. Some looks said, "That's disappointing. I thought you were better than that." Others were a little nod and smile, telling me, "Nice job, kid, keep it going." He was a natural leader and role model.

January to March 2002 was a very difficult time for my young family, but I followed the events of Johnny's death through my family and later through whatever online sources I could find, including watching the Medal of Honor ceremony. But I didn't know the whole story until reading your book. When I read his story, I was sad for your loss but not surprised by his heroics. He was always that guy. I just wanted to share this memory with you and keep his alive.

Thank you, Jimmy, for sharing this beautiful story. John echoed that same advice and words of encouragement years later when he was assigned his first subordinate to train after he became a Combat Controller. He had a keen sense of how others should be treated and why certain things happened the way they did.

Tom Allen has lived in Windsor Locks most of his life. He and his wife Diane have three boys who were brought up knowing all about John Chapman. Their eldest Michael John was named after John and his friend and fellow diver Michael DuPont, and Kevin and John are godparents to their middle son David. The story of Tom Allen and John Chapman began years before Tom had kids when John was in eighth grade.

Tom was working as a police officer when he volunteered to coach the Windsor Locks High School boys' diving team. Having been a diver in the past, he felt he could share his expertise with the team. Tom coached for twenty years, through a career change from police officer to Radiologic Technologist and the grueling hours it required. He brought out the best in every diver he coached and forged friendships with many of them and their families. Our family grew particularly close with him. Tom was introduced to the Chapman family when Kevin started diving during his freshman year. Kevin and another diver John Getz turned out to be Tom's top two divers; he had them practicing long and hard. John watched on occasion and went to the swim meets to cheer for best friends Kevin and Getz. (We called John Getz "John," but that will get too confusing, so I'm calling him Getz here. I mean no disrespect.)

I also dove for Tom when I was a freshman and Kevin was a junior. John was in eighth grade at the time, and he watched as Kevin, Getz, and I learned how to nail dive after dive on the one-meter springboard. The boys were much more aggressive than I was, and it caught John's attention. True to form, just as he had done in soccer, he decided he wanted to join us even though he was too young. He asked Coach Allen to let him join the practices, so Tom asked Dad what he thought about it. Dad commented, "He is the best athlete in the whole crew." And just like that, John became our unofficial teammate that year.

Since John had a season of diving practice under his belt before he ever became a Windsor Locks Raider, he had an edge over divers from other schools when he became a freshman. He developed a fast friendship with sophomore Michael DuPont. Seniors Kevin and Getz had John and Michael nipping at their heels, biding their time and waiting their turn.

Tom marveled at how well the four boys worked together. John and Mike bonded since they were the two "youngsters," and Kevin and Getz had been best friends all through high school. John Getz is legally blind, which made for some interesting times both on and off the diving board, but the boys ignored the disability. He could see a very short distance, though not clearly, if he tipped his head a certain way, but nothing stopped him; he was always up for the next challenge. Kevin even let Getz drive his moped a few times! He would ride on the back, telling him when and what direction to turn. They were nuts!

During that 1980 diving season, the two older boys showed Mike and John what they needed to do—accept that diving is repetitious and requires hours and hours of practice, many days a week. The boys took their diving mishaps in stride, from clipping the board with one body part or another to landing flat on the water, which is just as painful as landing flat on the ground. Trust me, I know! John never once backed away from a challenging dive; none of them did, and by the time they finished practice, it was common for their skin to be crimson red from smacking the water's surface during countless missed dives. None of the pains of diving made the boys shy away. Once they mastered the basic dives, and they *did* master them (they consistently received high scores for those dives), they moved on to more advanced dives. Learning those more difficult skills—inward dives, backward flips, one-and-a-half, two-and-a-half, twists— is where their skin really paid the blistering price. If they didn't head to the locker room looking like a freshly boiled lobster, Coach Allen knew they hadn't put in the effort that he wanted to see.

When four young men spend as much time together as they did, mischief is bound to happen. Sometimes, it was outside of practice, and sometimes they found ways to make practices a little more interesting. Michael remembers,

> I have to say that I was always a bit of an adrenaline junky but that fit in quite well with both Chapman brothers. We (Kevin, John, John Getz, and I) would frequently drive to Windsor High School to

go diving at night because they had a three-meter board. Kevin would drive his Subaru like he stole it, and we didn't always stay on the road. When we did, he would proceed to see how much air he could get over the railroad tracks on the way. We all laughed like hell and had a lot of fun. Windsor Locks High School was having some repairs done to the ceiling one year, and we got the bright idea to move the scaffolding over to the edge of the pool. All of us took turns flipping, diving, and jumping until Tom Allen walked in to see what we were doing and just about had a coronary. I think it was a good thing that we didn't have a trampoline at the school!

John and Michael had also developed a favorite diving challenge for themselves.

During practices, John and I would take turns diving between the swimmers because, naturally, we had practice at the same time. We thought it would be fun to time our dives closer and closer to the swimmers as they approached the deep end. Well, as you can guess, John dove about a foot in front of Duane Letentre, and the bubbles kept him from seeing the end of the pool. Needless to say, Duane and the swim coach, Coach Malone, were *not* happy with us, hence the trips to Windsor High!

Their diving escapades were not always indoors. Constantly on the lookout for different ways to challenge themselves, they discovered the Granby Gorge in nearby, Granby, Connecticut. It is a swimming area off Route 189, which includes a cliff that only the truly daring would attempt to jump off. It was calling their names. The highest part of the cliff is thirty-five to forty feet above the water, and entries had to be precise because the stream below has rocks and undercurrents that are ever-present dangers of the swimming hole. A rope hung on the water's edge so daredevil divers could pull themselves out, but there was no assistance for the climb back up to the top. Those who craved another adrenaline rush would have to free-climb the rocks, which were wet and slippery from other divers, to get to the jump-off point.

Though many people had suffered various injuries in the swimming hole—from cuts and scrapes to broken bones, to one fatality years before—it was a favorite spot for my two brothers and their crazy friends to test their mettle and tempt their fates. Most other visitors to the Granby Gorge cliff would jump feet first into the stream, but that wasn't risky enough for the boys. All four of them did the same dives from the cliff that they did off the diving boards. There were front flips and back flips, reverse dives and inwards; whatever they could imagine. While John and Michael helped Getz get into position at the jump-off point, Kevin dove in ahead of him to create bubbles on the water's surface. It was the only way he could see the water right before he hit. Anyone watching from a distance would never know one of them was legally blind. He did not need much help climbing back up either!

The last year all four boys dove together garnered quite a coup for the diving team. They all placed in the top seven. Michael should have been sixth, but Mom said some "hanky panky" was going on with the scoring; the judges wouldn't let her or Coach Allen see the lists. The standings brought attention to the diving team that it had not seen before. John and Michael were excited by their rankings but also were looking forward to the next year when *they* would be top dogs.

In October of 2018 at Hurlburt Field in Fort Walton Beach, Florida, the 24 held a dedication ceremony for the 24th SOW (Special Operations Wing) Building, renaming it after John. Kevin was asked to speak and he shared a memory from the year following his own graduation from high school, "I've been blessed to be very good at almost anything I try; John, on the other hand, was great at nearly everything. When I was a senior, I destroyed the highest long-standing record for springboard diving. The very next year as a sophomore, John destroyed *my* record and, in his humility, was distraught that I might be upset and apologized for breaking my record." Kevin's story is a testament that John never backed down from doing his best, but he also respected the efforts of others. He was fierce *and* fiercely loyal.

Over the three years that John and Michael were diving teammates, they pushed each other to reach for bigger and better dives. Tom only had to give them a little bit of guidance because their competitiveness and camaraderie pushed them harder than he ever could. "What I remember most about John," says Michael, "is his competitive drive and the inspiration he gave me while we were diving together

111

in high school. My favorite part about our friendship was during my senior year when we kept trading places on setting new records for diving. He broke the record first, then I would beat his record, and back and forth. I believe he still holds the record for highest score. We also took first and second place for the division and had a lot of fun at State. We smuggled a six-pack of St. Pauli Girl and drank it in your parent's van on the way back. I'm pretty sure we got into trouble for that too!"

Before their last season of diving together, Tom was approached by three area schools that didn't have dive coaches. They asked if he and his divers would be open to coaching and practicing together, even though they would be competing against one another. Tom agreed and Newington High, Windsor High, and Avon/ Simsbury High became a combined diving team of sorts—combined in practice, but competitors in meets. Diving is considered an individual sport, but John and Michael made it a team sport when they resolved to help some of the less-experienced divers. Being far more advanced than their new teammates, while Tom was coaching some, Michael and John worked with others, teaching them the basics of diving and fine-tuning what skills they had. Their efforts were rewarded that year because *all* of the kids made it to State, and Tom said, "They all learned the value of respect, sportsmanship, and cooperation." John and Michael were not only confident enough in themselves to accept practicing with competitors, but they also helped train them. Whether they realized it or not, teaching the others *had* to improve their own skills too.

John's four years of high school diving were years spent getting progressively better. His accomplishments never surprised me. As Mom recalls, "John placed fifth in the state championships in their class division his freshman year, third in his sophomore year, and first in his junior and senior years." His efforts in high school had him ranked #1 in college diving the following year. Since John's death, some have said he was a contender for the Junior Olympics. I'm not sure where that originated, but it is simply not true. Perhaps someone once said, "He is Junior Olympic caliber." That *is* true.

Thinking of John now, Michael simply said, "I miss him dearly and am very proud to have not only known him but to be a part of his and your families' lives. He is a true warrior in his sacrifice for our country."

The fearlessness, confidence, and perseverance required to be a great competitive diver are attributes John summoned many times in his life. One of those times also involved a dive, only this time it was from the bow of a ship in the dark. He and some of his CCT and PJ buddies were training with SEALs, including boarding a ship without anyone noticing. I was not told what type of ship they boarded, but, depending on whether it was loaded or not, the drop into the water could have been anywhere from forty to eighty feet! Once they were all on deck and gathered at the bow, one of the trainers said, "Ok, now everybody over the side." Looking at each other and wondering if they had heard right, the trainees were shocked when John climbed the rail at the bow, stood with arms straight out to the sides, took a deep breath, and pulled a full gainer (a reverse dive) into the darkness below. Mouths were agape for two reasons: 1) no one knew he could dive, and 2) the normal way off the bow is feet first. John quelled any fear he may have felt and went for it.

PART TWO

Civilian to Airman to Combat Control Pipeline and
John's Little Family

To live life to its fullest, seeing as you only live once.
~ John's yearbook plans for his future

12

Civilian

You will need to find your passion.
Don't give up on finding it because then all you're
doing is waiting for the Reaper.
~ Randy Pausch

When John graduated high school in June 1983, he originally wanted to go to Embry Riddle for Aeronautical Engineering but discovered it was much too expensive. The University of Connecticut (UConn) was the obvious choice, and he enrolled in engineering courses. He also joined the men's diving team, already ranked #1 in that division for the one-meter board, and #3 on the three-meter board. He thought his life was all planned out.

He attended the main campus in Storrs, Connecticut, with many of his high school classmates. David Wrabel continued his friendship with John as they began their freshman year at UConn. Living across campus from each other didn't keep them from finding a little mischief every now and again. David remembers,

John told me that Brian [Topor] had called, and they were having a toga party in his dorm at AIC [American International College] in Springfield [Massachusetts]. He said, "You gotta wear a toga," and I'm like, "What do I do?" John said, "Just get a sheet," so that's what I wore to AIC—a toga sheet and nothing else. John wore a toga too, so when we got to AIC and headed to Brian's dorm, which had a large population of big football players, I started noticing that we were the only people draped in bed sheets. Brian wasn't in his room, and the huge football guys were looking at us, making comments about stuff they'd like to do to us. At that point, I thought we were screwed because Brian was nowhere to be found, we had nothing on but togas, and these guys were pretty intent on scaring the shit out of us. So, while I was shuddering in a corner, not sure what to do or where Brian could be, John was just casually standing there in his toga and talking to them as if nothing was wrong. When we finally saw Brian round the corner at the end of the hall, I said, 'Oh, thank God!' He had no idea we were coming and, of course, there was no toga party. We must have had street clothes in the car, because the next thing I remember, John, Brian, and I were out drinking at some local bar. I could have killed John back then, but it's a memory that makes me laugh now and one that I will never forget. It was so John.

John's time at UConn was short. He was smart but, as it turned out, studying was not his "thing; *doing* was his thing. He and David excelled at finding ways to lower their GPAs, and after the first semester, John's grades had slipped to the point he was no longer eligible to dive. He knew college wasn't for him. As it became clearer to John and David that their freshman year was an educational bust, they drank beer and talked about what was next for them. John thought about joining the Air Force but wasn't quite sure yet. David had zero interest in joining the military, so he remained at UConn, adjusted his beer time, and earned his degree. Though their paths went in very different directions, they remained the best of friends, keeping in contact often over the years.

With his freshman year at UConn in the rearview mirror, John knew it would be his last year at any college—not that he couldn't do the work or that he couldn't succeed there, it was something more; his heart wasn't in it. He knew he wanted something different but wasn't quite ready to commit to a career in the Air Force. For the next year, he worked for Eddie Habermeier at Bradley Automotive Center on King Spring Road in Windsor Locks. John worked as a mechanic, learned how to fix dents and do other bodywork, and drove a tow truck. He liked the challenge of solving engine issues. Sometimes, the fix was easy, but other times, John was forced to use trial and error, mulling over the problem and thinking it through. And on rare occasions, the answer was "outside of the box."

John excelled at solving puzzles—mechanical or situational. He came up with unconventional solutions to seemingly unsolvable problems. Answers that would not occur to most people were obvious to him. He routinely made decisions on the fly, an enviable skill and one that served him well throughout his life.

On one occasion, he had to tow a customer's vehicle back to Boston. Bradley Automotive was a small operation with a couple of tow trucks, so John was given the older and more battered of the two. He didn't care; it moved and did the job. There's an old saying, "The carpenter's house is never finished." In this case, the mechanic's truck was not without flaws. It was old, it had dents and rust, the suspension was rough, and one of the headlights didn't work, but that old workhorse was heavy and mechanically sound.

John drove the beast to Boston, leaving after business hours. By the time he reached the city almost two hours away, night was creeping in. He dropped the customer's vehicle and got right back onto Interstate 90 headed for home. He was about halfway to Connecticut when he realized that the one good headlight had just crapped out. The interstate is well-lit, but he still needed headlights when he eventually left the highway, so he pulled over to set about fixing it. This will horrify some of you younger readers, but ... it was 1984; there was no such thing as cell phones and no random pay phone on the side of the interstate, so John had to rely on his wits. He went through the logical tests, but the old bulb had burned out, leaving him with no working headlights. John's solution was epic, and so John.

He recounted his adventure to me the next day, "At first, I didn't know what the hell I was going to do. It was a long walk to anywhere, and there weren't many cars passing by. Figured I had to do something, so I checked the truck and found one of those big-ass flashlights. You know, the ones that take a million D batteries? So, I took some rope and tied the light to the middle of the bumper as tight as I could get it. It wasn't going anywhere." I remember laughing as I pictured the scene, and John added as he laughed too, "I don't know how I made it all the way back to the garage. The truck bounced so much over bumps, especially once I left I-90 and my one, small light kept doing this." He gestured as if both hands were on the wheel and stuck in a rapid bouncing motion, nodding his head to the same rhythm as his hands to show how he and the light were mercilessly jostled about. He laughed his "this is really funny" cackle because it really was funny.

John learned a lot from Eddie, especially working on engines and the value of sticking with a problem. The answer would come eventually. He was fine-tuning his work ethic: If you're going to do it, take the time to do it right. Mom remembered one occasion that shocked Eddie but solidified his confidence in John's ability.

One day, Eddie told him to do a fender repair on this car. He said, "I don't want you using any new stuff; you just work this one." Later, Eddie went back and said, "Damn it, John! I told you not to use a brand-new fender on this!" And Johnny said, "I didn't." Eddie was amazed; he was checking the whole thing out so closely and he couldn't even tell that it wasn't a brand-new fender. Previous to that, he would only let Johnny work on older cars that had a fender accident or other body parts, but once he saw the quality of John's work, he was working on the expensive cars that would come in with damages.

John's commitment and attention to detail proved to Eddie and to himself that nothing was impossible. The work ethic he brought to the job was evident on one tow truck run into Massachusetts. Mom recounts what happened that day.

> He was up in the Springfield area. He went to a repair on a highway, and as he was hooking up, he came up with his head and hit part of the hook and really gashed his head. But he finished the job, towed it back to the shop, and when he came home, there was all this crusted, dried blood on his head and I said, "John, we have to take you in and get stitches," because it was a nasty gash. But he finished his job. He didn't wimp out because he was bleeding all over the place. He just came home kind of bloody-looking.

When John was working for Eddie, he'd stop by my apartment in the tow truck every once in a while. His visits always made my day even though they were usually pretty short, and we'd talk about whatever came to mind. I miss those times.

As young adults, Kevin and John would head to northern Michigan to hunt with our dad and Uncle Dale on occasion. After John joined the Air Force, he went as often as he could. In the same October 2018 speech at Hurlburt Field when Kevin talked about John beating his diving record, he remembered a particular hunting event that has stayed with him all these years.

> We were walking through the woods, enjoying each other's company, and having some good conversation when we walked into a clearing. We both spotted this huge doe a good distance out, but she also spotted us and was keeping an eye on us. We could not move much, lest we spook her. While it would be easy to argue over who took the shot, that was not who John was. Not only did he insist that I take the shot, but because of the distance, he volunteered to be my bipod in order to ensure a steady shot. John esteemed me more than himself.

This reminds me of John and soccer: It didn't matter who got the goal, it only mattered that his team scored. In this case, he gave the shot to Kevin, happily making the assist.

Listening to Kevin's hunting story reminded me of something John told me after he became a Combat Controller. He was an excellent marksman, including great accuracy from long distances. After hunting another time in Michigan, John returned to his home in North Carolina empty-handed. I called to hear how the trip went, and he laughed before launching into his tale, "Well, there I was, waiting patiently for a deer to come my way when I spotted a buck not too far away. I didn't want to miss the shot, but I got so excited at how big he was that I forgot to take my time and breathe, and I squeezed off a round way too soon." He laughed again, only this time it was that cackle I loved, and I could almost hear him shaking his head at himself. "I tried to get a bead on him again, but that first hurried shot scared him off. I missed my chance at a huge buck because I made a rookie mistake." I laughed with him and bet myself that he would never rush a shot again, nor would he miss.

13

Airman

When you go beyond yourself, that's when magical things can happen.
~ MSgt Roger Sparks, author of *Warrior's Creed*

John's interest in auto body and mechanical work never waned, but he realized it wasn't his dream job. He resurrected thoughts about joining the Air Force because he felt a pull to do something more—something exciting—and he wanted to share his decision with us. He had thought about joining the Coast Guard if the Air Force didn't pan out, but the Air Force was his first choice. He sought Dad's input first. The portion of Dad's letter to the 24 that is relevant to John's decision follows.

He learned a very good lesson as I attested to by later events. The next summer, in the third week of August, he came to me again. "Dad, I want to join the Air Force." I looked at him and asked, "What about college?" He didn't want to go back to college but wanted to enter the Air Force. I told him, "It is a good thing to go into the military, but don't waste it; come out with a skill that you can use the rest of your life for hobby or sustenance." He said, "Thanks, Dad, because I joined up on the first of August and report on the third of September."

Dad was not surprised that John had already made his decision before talking with him. He understood that, although John would come to him for advice, he was confident enough to make life choices on his own. John did not join the Air Force alone. Danny Walsh, brother of kindergarten street fighter Maureen, remembers it well.

I met John in second grade. We grew up in the same neighborhood and were pretty close as kids. He was always a bit crazy, but in a good way, and very fun to hang out with. He was the only person I ever met who made playing the accordion cool. He played soccer, and I played football, so we grew apart in later years, but we remained friends and hung out from time to time throughout high school and our first semester of college. We met up while he was working at Bradley Auto, and he told me he realized the Air Force would be a better fit for him, and he talked me into joining with him. On August 1, 1985, we went together and signed up. Since we went for different careers, and our schooling started at different times, I didn't realistically think we would ever be stationed together, so I was very surprised to find him at Lowry AFB when I got there in 1986, but that's a whole other story!

The next stop was Mom. How was she going to take his news? When John spoke with her, she supported his decision. Dad had been in the Air Force for three years, and even though it was before they married, she had a tiny glimpse into what the Air Force could offer. She hoped John had found his passion but also was concerned that he might choose a dangerous career path. She asked him to try a safe path first. John promised he would.

After speaking with our parents, he stopped by my apartment. As he pulled into my driveway, I was getting ready to change the oil in my car and he grinned. He made no move to help me, respecting the lessons taught by Dad. In order for any of us kids to get a driver's license, we had to know how to change a tire, change the oil, change the air filter, and grease the front end. Instead of offering to help, John pulled up some pavement and dove into why he had stopped by. "I don't feel that being a mechanic is what I want to do forever. I love working on cars but not as a career." I was ready to drain the oil, so I positioned the tub under the oil pan nut, turned it, and watched the oil flow out. Satisfied that the oil stream would stay in the tub, I crawled from under my car, and we stood to talk. He looked squarely at me, watching for my reaction, and said, "I'm joining the Air Force. I need to do something more than stay in Windsor Locks my whole life. I want to see the world if they let me. I can't stay here." I thought for a moment before responding, "Yeah, I know. I've noticed you're getting restless. I never would have guessed the Air Force, but I am happy for you, and I am so very proud. You'll do great!" And I knew he would. He was smart and driven and not afraid to test himself.

John didn't need my blessing; he had already made his decision, but I think he felt that telling us in person was the right thing to do. It would not be easy to watch him leave, but I knew he needed to go. John's decision to join the Air Force eventually allowed him to experience everything he had dreamed about as a kid, and so much more.

After speaking with all of us, he went to see Tom and Diane Allen, our dive coach, and his wife. The three of them sat around the dining table, and John told them his plans. When they asked what his family thought, he told them we supported his decision but Mom was concerned about his career field. He told them that he had promised to stay in a safe career. After hearing him out, Tom and Diane also gave their approval. Tom was an Air Force veteran, so he knew the benefits that lay ahead for John if he chose to take advantage of them.

John spent the rest of August 1985 completing tasks at Bradley Automotive and spending time with friends he wouldn't see after he left for Basic Training. On September 2, 1985, he and a kid from Rocky Hill stayed in a hotel in Springfield, waiting for departure the following day from Bradley Airport to Lackland AFB in San Antonio, Texas. John had an idea of what lay ahead at Basic Training and was mentally prepared for it. One of the first prerequisites was the oh-so-stylish buzz cut. He sat down and said goodbye to most of his locks. As his thick, brown hair fell to the floor, the scar just above his hairline emerged. It was one of several souvenirs from childhood. He earned it in high school when he and Duane Letendre were messing around on the starting blocks at the shallow end of the pool. Duane reminded John of a silly dive he used to do off the blocks years before and dared him to do it again. Never one to say, "No, I can't," John dove right in, only it didn't go exactly as before. With no hesitation after the dive, John swam to the other end of the pool, leaving a giant trail of blood all the way down the lane. He had hit the bottom of the pool and split his head wide open. About thirty stitches later, John's wound was closed and so were any further attempts at that dive, at least not in the shallow end. When the stitches needed to be removed, the doctor missed half of them. Instead of going back, John had Mom take out the remaining stitches. He wanted to memorialize his fresh Basic Training buzz-cut and his newly unveiled scar, so he went to a photo booth and printed the strip of photos. He cut off one of the tiny squares and sent it to Mom. She still has it.

Before heading to basic training, John had not played sports for at least a year, so he wasn't in top physical shape, but he was still slim and strong and knew they would whip him into shape. As one of the "old guys," he was twenty years old and most of the other recruits were eighteen and fresh out of high school, he quickly became a leader among his peers and an assigned leader in his flight. John was part of Squadron 3707, Flight 189.[4]

---

[4] We have tried to find a photo of his graduating flight, to no avail. I would like to request that if anyone out there was in his flight, graduating in November or December of 1985, and you have the graduation photo and/or photos of him during that time, it would mean the world if you could contact me and share that which has eluded me thus far. And I thank you in advance. theloloproject24@gmail.com.

After his two-month basic training and before reporting to his assignment at Lowry AFB in Aurora, Colorado, John went home for a quick visit. He showed Mom a pamphlet that all male recruits at basic training received for Air Force Combat Control and Pararescue. John was intrigued and excited by what they told him, and he wanted to try that career path. Mom was not convinced and again made him promise to at least try something less dangerous. John agreed to remain an Information Systems Tech, at least for a while. Somewhat deflated but determined to do his best, John headed to Aurora and settled into his new life as an airman.

His career field kept him in front of a computer all day, every day. It was not the perfect job for him, but his promise to Mom kept him "chained to the desk." He found interests outside of work, one of which was his baby, the Pontiac LeMans that high school friend Jim "Guppie" Guthrie sold to him after much insistence from John. He spent hours keeping the body clean and the engine tuned. His attitude toward the upkeep of a vehicle began many years prior as he explained in a second-grade writing assignment. It is entitled "My Three Wishes."

One day I was walking along the street, and I found a bottle. I opened it and smoke came out of it. I heard a voice. It said, "Do you want wishes?" The first wish was for a bike. I rode it each day. I liked it too. I washed it. I kept it clean. It was a good bike. The second wish was a sizzler, and it went fast. I liked it. I kept it nice. It was so fast you couldn't even see it. The third wish was a Hot Wheel. I put it on the track and it went fast. I kept it snazzy. I kept the track clean when I put the Hot Wheel on the track. I liked those wishes and kept them forever. The End.

All of his vehicles were pristine, and he proudly took a picture of the Le Mans in front of an Air Force B-52 that was on display at Lowry AFB. It's a classic "military memory" photo.

About two years before John died, Rachel and I went to visit Valerie and him during spring break. I called him when I reached a certain spot in North Carolina so he knew he would see us in two hours. Well, I made it in less than an hour and a half and even he was impressed, saying, "Holy shit. You must have been flying to get here *that* fast." Lead-footing does run in the family. It was around midnight, so we said quick hellos and went to bed. When I got up late the next day, John was washing my car inside and out. He had already checked the fluid levels and topped off the oil. He told me I should get new tires; bare tires were normal for me because I couldn't afford new ones. I felt guilty that he was servicing my car while I slept in, but he loved doing it.

John was a good-looking guy. He was a lean 5'10" with an athletic build, thick brown hair, and blue eyes that made girls swoon. He was young, smart, funny, and fun to be around, but I knew he was having problems in one area of his life—women. He couldn't figure out why no girl came into his life and stayed. He was a good catch, so what was the deal? He wasn't desperate for a girlfriend but would have liked it if he had one. We used to talk quite a bit on the phone when he was in Aurora, and he occasionally lamented to me about his love life woes. Honestly, I was as stumped as he because he really was a great guy—very loyal, romantic, and thoughtful. I assured him that he would find "the one" someday, and in the meantime, not to worry about it.

John wasn't necessarily stressing, but I could tell it bothered him—enough so that he came up with ways to better his odds. He told me that he was hosting a party that weekend and asked for a recipe of mine. It wasn't surprising that he would have friends over, but I asked him, "What's the occasion?" He giggled and said, "I'm having a *Princess House®* party." I laughed out loud before saying, "*Princess House®*? Now *that's* funny!" I mocked him for having a girly party. (*Princess House®* is a direct-sales company that sells hand-blown and lead crystal glassware at home parties.) John waited for me to stop teasing him and said, "Think about it. Who goes to *Princess House®* parties? Women! And the more the merrier!" He laughed at his brilliance, and I was impressed with his clever ruse. I wished him luck, not that he needed it. John hosted a couple of those parties while he was in Aurora, and it is quite likely that he was rewarded with a date or two at the very least.

When John was three months into his assignment at Lowry, he received a phone call from Danny Walsh, the buddy who joined the Air Force with him. Danny had just arrived at Lowry and had been given the briefing on how to conduct himself as a graduate of basic training and tech school. "For the first two weeks, you will *always* wear your uniform, you will *not* leave the base, and you will *not* drink alcohol. For the second two weeks, you will *always* wear your uniform, you may leave the base, but you will *not* drink alcohol." When John heard him repeating the orders, he interrupted, "Yeah, yeah. Pack some civilian clothes in a bag and meet me at the gym." John and Danny got shitfaced off base on the first day of his assignment and they spent many more similar days during the next five months until Danny was sent elsewhere. Is anyone truly surprised?

John joined the Lowry base soccer team and became friends with one of his teammates David Klein. The team traveled to other bases, and one of those away games coincided with Tammy's plan to visit John in the spring of 1986. She flew to Arizona to watch the game then joined him on the drive back to Colorado. When David first saw Tammy, he thought she was too young, mostly because of how she dressed—cute top, skirt, and ankle socks in high-top Reeboks. When he found out she was actually nineteen, a happy David began showing interest in her. To Tammy's delight, he was one of John's passengers on the trip home. John and Tammy spent lots of time with David during her visit, and the undeniable attraction continued after she returned to Connecticut. During a Father's Day call to his dad, David told him, "I've met the one I'm going to marry." They were married in September 1986 and, thirty-eight years later are still each other's best friend.

John was excited to have family close by, and it didn't take long before the word *in-law* was dropped and David became *brother*. John's boredom at work was somewhat alleviated as the three spent countless weekends and holidays together.

By the time John was accepted to try out for the Combat Control pipeline, Tammy and David had moved to Colorado Springs so David could pursue higher education. During his time left at Lowry, John traveled south to Colorado Springs as often as he could. It's about an hour down I-25 to get there from Aurora, and John usually made it in just over a half hour. See? Lead-footing *is* a family thing!

On a trip I made to Colorado, John drove the four of us to Cripple Creek in his granny-tan, two-door LTD. It ran great but was not very pretty. Back then, Cripple Creek was truly a one-horse town (or one-donkey town) right out of an old spaghetti western movie. It is at an altitude of almost 9,700 feet, and getting there was a harrowing drive, especially when John was behind the wheel. We traveled up a narrow, steep, and winding dirt road with a wall of rock on one side and a drop-off into tall pines on the other. The road did not have a guardrail, so one wrong move and we'd be doing a *Thelma and Louise* off the side of the mountain. As John and David laughed loudly in the front seat, Tammy and I were tossed around in the back, convinced we would skid off the road and fly into the abyss of the Colorado wilderness. We didn't, but John had good fun making us think we might!

During his last months in Aurora, John met an elderly couple who lived in Florissant, a tiny town about forty-five minutes west of Colorado Springs. He loved them, and Tammy shared how they met.

> John was dating a young woman at the time, and she introduced him to her grandparents Harold and June. We spent time with John and his girlfriend, hiking at Garden of the Gods or just hanging out, so David and I got to meet Harold and June as well. Harold wasn't well—he was on oxygen—and June wasn't in the best of health either. They lived in the mountains north of *Florissant Fossil Beds National Monument* and had many projects around their home that were difficult for Harold to do.

John, a single, handsome, fun, twenty-one-year-old airman, chose to spend many of his weekends at their home, chopping and stacking wood for them to have during the winter months, and finishing a fence that Harold started but wasn't able to complete. Tammy and David often joined him on his trips to their home so they could help this sweet couple with whom they, too, were smitten. Tammy continued:

> Even after John and his girlfriend broke up, he continued to visit them without her. I don't know if John kept in touch with them after he left Aurora, but when David and I were at his funeral, we saw flowers that Harold and June had sent. Harold passed that same year in November.

Of the time spent at the home in the mountains, David shared, "That's where I helped John make his dining table. It was made out of oak; it was beautiful. A few years later, when John brought it to Okinawa, three years of intense humidity destroyed it." That wasn't the end of it, though. About a year after John was killed, Valerie gave that sad table to my husband Kenny who then salvaged what he could to make a three-tiered corner shelf. He remembers, "The table was pretty warped, so there was quite a bit of unusable wood. I used every bit of the good wood to create the shelves, and it's thinner than the one I made for our home because I had to do a lot of sanding." The transformed table now hangs in Mom's living room, displaying family photos and treasured items.

When John could have been back in Aurora partying or doing what young airmen do, he instead chose to spend time with Harold and June, listening to their stories, and soaking up their knowledge. He had long since figured out that he could learn a great deal just by listening to people who had "been there"—wherever "there" was.

Dad and I were talking a little after John died, reminiscing about how he loved talking with elderly people, especially old military guys. I told him about an encounter John had at an airport. With an hour or two delay between flights, he spent the entire time listening to the stories of a World War II or Vietnam veteran. That reminded Dad of his own experience during a visit from John.

We were walking the aisles of the local *Meijer* when John walked away to use the bathroom. I expected him to return and spent the better part of a half hour looking for him. I finally decided we would meet up at some point, so I checked out and went to wait for him outside. I looked to my right as I went through the exit door and found John sitting on a bench, shooting the breeze with an old World War II veteran. He was smiling and hanging on every word the man uttered.

We should all be as insightful as John in recognizing that older generations *want* to share with us and would love the opportunity. They would also enjoy the company however short it is. In 2000 or 2001, John was on TDY in Virginia Beach when he called Mom. She told him that Grandma Kennedy was there with her walking group; they were elderly ladies who walked about three miles together every morning, rain or shine. Occasionally, they went on weekend trips, and this one landed them not far from John. He called Grandma and arranged to take her to dinner. When he returned her to the hotel, she said, "I want you to meet my friends." It was late so most of the ladies, all in their 70s and 80s, were in one room, clad in their pajamas and robes. They were playing a dice game called Farkle and invited John to join them. John and his entourage of little old ladies spent the evening drinking wine, playing Farkle, and having a grand time. They giggled when John made the name of the game sound like flatulence, "Oh, you farkled!" He had so much fun with Grandma and her friends, and they fell in love with him.

Go talk to an old veteran; spend time with your grandma. You may be surprised by what you learn, and you may also find you get just as much out of the encounter as they do if not more.

14

Combat Control Pipeline

First There.
~ Combat Control motto

John continued plugging along in his Information Systems job but was feeling the itch again. He knew he had to find something else—something more meaningful, more challenging. He loved a challenge. He hadn't forgotten about the recruitment visit at basic training, nor could he ignore the Combat Control pamphlet squirreled away in his drawer, so he assigned himself a mission: Gather as much information as he could about Combat Control. The more he read, the more he was sure it was what he wanted to do. The added bonus was, if successful, he'd get to play with all kinds of gadgets, vehicles, and man toys. It was a huge departure from desk jockeying and would be completely against what he had promised Mom, but he became passionate about trying to make it through the pipeline—the rigorous and exhausting training that goes into becoming an elite Air Force Combat Controller.

He looked over the pamphlet again, contemplating the information it gave. The pipeline is the longest and most difficult of all Special Operations Forces entry training—with the most intense course at the front end: the dreaded INDOC (Combat Control Indoctrination Course). In the 1990s, the washout rate at INDOC was over 90%—out of 120 men who started, twelve *might* make it through. Trainees who survived and graduated INDOC then had eighteen more months of training ahead of them—physically punishing and mentally taxing— and failure at any juncture could send them packing. John was not dissuaded. The Combat Control mission intrigued him. While Combat Controllers are experts in countless aspects of warfare (and even participate in humanitarian missions), their main skill sets are controlling the airspace above battlegrounds, operating austere airfields, pinpointing enemy targets, and calling in airstrikes. Many times, they are called on to seize and control airfields, or create ones where none exist. To call in airstrikes, or to set up an airstrip, these brave men are inserted to a mountaintop, to a valley, or to a hostile environment before any other ground troops arrive. They are truly "first there."

His mind made up, John submitted the request to cross-train into Special Tactics. He was excited and nervous but wanted it like he had never wanted anything before.

Dad visited after his request was sent and John told him about what would hopefully become his new career field. In his letter to the 24, Dad addressed that decision and how John told him:

A year later, I visited him at his base near Denver, Colorado. He again sat down with me and asked what I thought about him changing his field to Combat Control in the Special Operations Forces. I knew he had already applied but decided to play his game. I asked what Combat Control consisted of, and he told me as best he could to enlighten me. I asked why he wished to go into this field. His comment was computers day in and day out bored him. He wanted to get into some action. I told him, "Go, get into it, but do the best job you can muster.

He had Dad's approval, though he knew he didn't need it. What would everyone else think? After Dad returned home to Michigan (he moved back after he and Mom divorced in 1986), John took leave and flew home to Connecticut. The conversation with Mom didn't go as calmly as it had with Dad. It wasn't unexpected. He *had* promised he would try to stay out of high-risk career fields. John told Mom that he felt he had fulfilled his promise to her; he tried a low-risk career and was miserable and restless. Mom was apprehensive but was also more understanding than he had expected. She agreed that he had kept his promise and gave him the blessing he didn't need but sought, nonetheless. She did ask him about the likelihood of something bad happening. He replied, "Well, the longer you play the odds, the more likely something will happen." No truer words.

When John came to talk with me, he already knew I would support him. We sat in my living room, talking over a drink. He started, "Well, I'm going to change my career field. I just can't sit all day in front of a computer anymore." I didn't ask questions; I just let him talk. "I didn't join the Air Force to be a glorified telephone operator. I want excitement. I want to make a difference. So, I am trying to get into the Combat Control training pipeline." I had never heard of Combat Control and had no idea that there even was such a thing as Air Force Special Tactics. He didn't tell me much about what his job would entail if he succeeded, and I didn't ask. His eyes sparkled as he told me about changing career fields. Seeing him happy was all that mattered, and I was blissfully oblivious to what he was signing up to do.

As was his ritual every time he was home, he stopped in to see Tom and Diane Allen, and this visit was no different. He found Tom in the backyard, tending the lawn. John and Tom had kept in close contact over the years since John left high school. Tom was family—someone he could bounce ideas off and, more importantly, someone who would always give it to him straight. After the usual greetings, John jumped right in and said, "You know, I gotta talk to you. I want a career change." Tom said, "Ok," letting the word hang between them, waiting for John to continue. "Well, I want to become a Combat Controller." Tom was well aware of what Combat Control was. He thought about John's revelation for a moment and then carefully said, "Oh, John, you gotta understand that our life expectancy in that is not very good." John looked seriously at Tom as he responded, "I understand that, but it's something I think I need to do." Tom remained reticent and again carefully chose his words, "You know I'm really reluctant to go along with it. Do your mom and dad know?" John nodded,

"Yeah, I talked to them." Tom was curious, "What are their thoughts?" John told Tom, "They're not too happy about it either," but he remained determined. After some thought, Tom finally said, "You know, John, I've trusted you all of these years and it's your choice. I'll back whatever you finally decide to do, but you have to understand that I know Diane will be reluctant, too, about this." John could only repeat, "It's what I really want to do." It took only a moment for Tom to respond, "Well, alright then."

John said they would be visited by investigators to interview them about whether they thought he could handle the career field. On the day of the interview, Tom and Diane sat across their dining room table from two agents. They asked all sorts of questions, including if they believed he had any kind of issues that should be brought to light. Tom and Diane answered honestly, "He's as straight as they come. Dedicated. He would put in any amount of time when he was learning how to dive with his brother and two buddies, and whatever it took to succeed, that's what John was going to do. He was noted for being friendly among individuals in school. He played multiple sports. Athletically, he was probably top in his class and even top in school history because of his athletic abilities." They told the agents that John was someone who would go out of his way to help another, no matter who they were. They told them about our disabled neighbor Mary Tersavich and how John "used to spend a tremendous amount of time with her, helping her color. To someone who didn't know, they'd think she and John were sister and brother because he displayed such love and affection for her."

Tom made it clear that John was "dedicated to people and had a love for people." He recounted his conversation with John and said, "I totally support him. This is what he wants to do, and I can guarantee you this is something he will be excellent at. There's nothing he can't do once he puts his mind to it, and he has a sense of what's right." Tom told them about how John stepped in to protect the underclassmen in high school. "He didn't think twice about it. That's the way he is. If you're under duress, he's coming to help." Indeed.

John's pipeline request was granted on June 6, 1989, and he never looked back. He returned to Lackland AFB to begin the hellish INDOC. The evaluations and training took place at OL-H (Operating Location H) where applicants discovered whether they had what it takes. John's personal time became coveted once he arrived at Medina, so phone calls were even less frequent than before. During some conversations with me, John shared his fear that he might not make it. It was extremely difficult, perhaps more than he anticipated. Even when he admitted that he was struggling, he always ended the conversation with, "But I'm not giving up."

Many years after John died, I was given a packet of John's INDOC documents, and as I read through them, it offered insight into just how difficult it was. The brother who I thought could do *anything* with ease truly did struggle. One document titled "Swim Training Record of Counseling" was written by John. He wrote, "Failed to relax in the water. Couldn't keep buddy calm, and it spread to me when I couldn't get air."

The rest of the seven records were written by trainers. One was a security violation because he left his watch unsecured. Another, written by TSgt Steve Rodman, was pretty stern.

> Today during crossovers, you delayed getting off the wall. You did not 'go' immediately when told to crossover. This will not be tolerated! If you continue to delay and not go day after day, training session after training session, you will not graduate this course, let alone meet the eval criteria. I recommend you evaluate your mental abilities again and prove you have what it takes to graduate from this course.

Sounds harsh, but it's all part of the weeding-out process. The last page in the counseling section made me laugh. It is written by TSgt Mike Mahoney and he wrote, "Get your shit together Chapboy. There is no excuse for not doing perfect knots. Now without further ado, I want you to begin chanting the phrase, 'I am a lick toad.' Continue this ritual 100 times or until I tell you to stop. Begin now!" These records show cracks in John's confidence, but he never gave up.

After a "down and out" call in 1989, I sent him a "survival kit." With little money to spare, I found a cigar box and filled it with goodies that were meant to make him smile. I stuffed it full of mints and gum; there was a deck of cards, and among other little items, a strand of condoms. I wanted to make him laugh. Had I known that all of their packages were inspected before they got them, I may have thought twice about at least one item, or maybe not.

John sent me a postcard after receiving his kit:

Dear Sis,

Thanks for the survival kit. It helps more than you know. Its things like that that make me laugh and my days here aren't so tough. The guys here got a chuckle out of it and wanted one of there own. I told them they would have to just go out and get there own sister to treat them as special as you treat me. Having family like you makes this Hell HOLE just a little bit barable. 10 Nov is my graduation. 3 more hard weeks and I am out of here and off to scuba school down in Key West. I finally see myself making it!

Love
John

I was so happy to read the last line of the postcard. It meant John had conquered his insecurity about making it and was charging full steam ahead.

He surprised me with another short letter not long after the postcard. In it, he expressed a tempered confidence, but confidence nonetheless. He wrote, "Five weeks of hard training are now complete with three to go. Just three more weeks and I'm out of here. I'm finally at a point where I can see myself passing this course. Although, it's not over yet, and I can't think too far ahead. I must concentrate on what I am doing. I don't want to blow it now." He ended with, "P.S. Most items have been used from my survival kit, but not all. I can only hope. Haha."

Though I didn't understand exactly what John was training to do or what the "pipeline" was all about, I did know John's tenacity and was sure he would succeed—where there's a will there's a way. I liked when he shared some of the training he was enduring, and I was sometimes shocked by things he was learning or what he had to endure—like when he was in a Washington State survival school "prison camp" in the middle of winter. He was stripped naked and put into a small, outdoor "cell" to give him an idea of what could happen to him should he ever be captured. The men were also shown how their actions could be used as propaganda against the US. It sounded tough—very tough. My confidence in John never once wavered even when his did. I was so freaking proud of him.

Toward the end of the pipeline in 1990, John sent me an Easter card from Keesler AFB, in Biloxi, Mississippi. He updated me on how well he was doing, and it was clear that the light was finally shining brightly at the end of his tunnel.

Mom and Dad attended John's graduation at Pope AFB in North Carolina. As a single mom working two jobs, I couldn't go. I will always regret missing his graduation. In hindsight, I should have taken a page out of John's book of life and just taken the time off, consequences be damned. Regardless, it was July 1990, and John had done it! He had accepted the challenge of becoming an Air Force Combat Controller, and although he stumbled a bit along the way, he finally earned the coveted red beret worn by Controllers. When he started the pipeline, he was one of over 100 men trying to see if they had what it took to hang with the big boys. In the end, the graduating class of 1990 was seven men strong, and only two were from John's original class. Perseverance, tenacity, humility, humor, confidence, and teamwork: these are but a few character traits needed to survive the Combat Control pipeline to become one of a very, very small and elite group. John proved that he had them all.

More from Dad's letter to the 24, discussing John's completion of the pipeline and graduation into Combat Control.

> Little did I know the word *muster* was going to play such a part in his getting to the end of the training pipeline. You folks know what he went through to get to be one of you and, ultimately, be able to don the coveted red beret. Some of you may have seen me there for him when he finished the pipeline. Then, of course, I was there for his graduation into Combat Control. Proud, you bet. Yes, he faltered

going through and started over; in the end, he was one of seven that made it through.

Though bittersweet, nothing would have kept Mom and Dad from sharing John's accomplishments with him. They were so very proud that he had earned his way through the longest and most intensive training pipeline in the world. They were glad that, although he almost failed, he pushed himself to overcome and succeed. They knew no matter what he was ordered to do, he would do it the best he could. But they also knew he would be in real-world situations from that day forward. John knew the risks, too, and he never looked back.

15

Family Life—Valerie, Madison and Brianna

The greatest thing a father can do for his daughter is to love her mother.
~ Elaine S. Dalton

John moved to Fayetteville, North Carolina, for the final phase of CCT school and was assigned to Pope after graduation. He bought a condo and a Harley Davidson Softail. John *loved* his Hog—and embraced the exhilaration of his new career. A month after John donned his scarlet beret, his friend Joe Puricelli, an Army 82nd Airborne paratrooper, invited him to visit Joe's hometown in western Pennsylvania for the weekend. John said, "Sure, why not?" After making the eight-hour drive to Windber, the two stopped to get gas and ran into a childhood friend of Joe's. Her name was Valerie Novak. John took an instant interest in her and the three of them hung out the rest of the night together. At some point, late into the evening, Joe left John and Val and the two talked into the wee hours of the morning. She remembered, "I dropped him off the next morning at Joe's mom's house, and Joe was like, 'So, how'd it go?' I told him, 'Well, we . . . are pretty good. We like each other.'"

John and Val dated long-distance. It was 1990; there was no email or cell phones, so they had to kick it "old school" through letters and hours-long phone calls. Valerie laughed as she recalled, "Sometimes my phone bill was like $200, and my dad would say, 'Have you seen this phone bill?'" Luckily for her, she had just graduated nursing school, had landed a good job, and was able to pay him back every time he received a shocking bill.

Jim Novak, Valerie's dad, took an immediate liking to John, which may have sealed the deal for her. I spoke with her about the early days of their courtship, and even all these years later, she is amazed at the effect John had on her dad.

> My dad never talks to anybody. He's very quiet, you know my dad. The first time he met John, oh my gosh! They were like best buds. It was . . . I was (makes a questioning face) and my mom was (makes a questioning face) . . . "He's talking. To a guy," and he just instantly took to John. He never talked to any of my former boyfriends. John made my dad, who is an extreme introvert, feel very comfortable with him. It was amazing; they had a great relationship. That always amazed me, and when John came home, man, he would talk to my dad about anything. My dad just loved the pieces out of him. John would say, "Hey Jim, what's going on?" and he'd be looking at the lawnmower.

And then, *of course*, there were the cars. My dad always worried about our vehicles— whether they were maintained and safe. Once I married John, I never got a phone call. He never worried about my vehicles again. But it was just amazing how my dad had this connection. John knew how to make him feel comfortable, and he would talk to him, which, still to this day, blows my mind.

It was apparent that Jim loved John like a son. He truly is a quiet and kind man, and the handful of times I got to witness their interactions validated the closeness they shared. Jim lit up when John was around, and the love and respect he had for him was reciprocated in full.

Valerie's mom Rita is the opposite of Jim. She loves to have fun, and she reveled in claiming John as a co-conspirator in forays on the town, especially to a favorite sub shop. Rita considered John her second son, and John loved her right back. They were two peas in a pod when they were together.

After a year of dating and wanting to honor the relationship he had with Jim, John drove to Windber in 1991 to ask him for Val's hand in marriage. Yeah, it was old-fashioned, but it was right, and Jim immediately approved. Valerie returned home from work and was surprised to see John at the house. "What are you doing here? I didn't know you were coming." John played it off as though he just missed her and wanted to visit. "He asked me to take him to Gravity Hill, a fun location not far from Windber where you put your car in neutral, foot off the brake, and it rolls uphill. I didn't really want to go there that evening but agreed since he had come all that way to see me. Once there, he popped the question. I wasn't entirely surprised; we had already talked about it, but the time and place *did* take me off guard."

Valerie accepted, and a year later they were married in a Catholic ceremony that culminated with a reception to beat them all. As the time drew near for them to leave, a polka song played loudly, and people on the dance floor surrounded Valerie. John was by the exit door with his best man Joe Maynor, the only other CCT graduate from their original class at Medina. I had no idea what was going on; it was nothing I had ever seen before. Having been briefed ahead of time, John and Joe "fought" their way to the center of the circling crowd so John could rescue Valerie. Then Joe parted the people while John carried her out the door to their waiting limo.

I didn't even realize what was going on until they were gone! I blame it on "mommy brain;" I'd just had my daughter four months earlier. When John got to see her before the wedding, he held her high in his arms so he could gaze into her beautiful, blue, almond-shaped eyes and declared, "If anyone ever hurts this little girl . . . ,"[5]and I had no doubt he would have followed through.

Immediately after they were married, John and Val made their home at Kadena AFB on the island of Okinawa, Japan. It was a three-year assignment, and Dad and our

---

[5] The rest of what John said is purposely withheld.

stepmom Tess were the only ones able to visit them because the rest of us couldn't manage it. And though John and Valerie really couldn't afford to fly back to the States either, they did come back once. "It was within a year of being there and, for us to travel back, it took a lot of John's time and money, but my brother was getting married, and it meant the world to me to be there. So, he made sure that we had the money and took the time, and we flew back home [to Pennsylvania] and got to see my brother get married." We didn't see John and Valerie during that visit, but lots of cards, letters, and videos were passed around to keep in contact as much as possible.

After settling into their new home, Valerie took a job with the hospital as John continued his training on the island and elsewhere. In some of the videos he shared, it was obvious they were enjoying their new adventure, traveling to other countries, eating funky food, exploring, camping, and everything there is to do on a new assignment.

John had always loved getting dressed up for Halloween and, luckily for him, so did Valerie. One year, Val wanted to be Medusa but couldn't find enough rubber snakes. Mom went on the hunt for them, going from store to store (this was before the Internet, people), and shipped them out right away. John was Dracula, and they scared the crap out of a young neighbor. Valerie remembers, "He hid behind the couch until he could be coaxed back out after being convinced it was 'Mr. John and Miss Valerie.'" She laughed as she remembered their first Halloween in Japan, "We dragged our kitchen table outside, he got a bunch of little wiener things and fake blood and a big ole knife, and pretended he was Igor from the Hunchback of Notre Dame. He was out there "chopping off his fingers with blood" and scared all the Okinawan kids away from our house. They would come on base to trick-or-treat, but after John scared them, they were afraid to go knock on our neighbors' doors! We had so much fun at Halloween. John friggin' loved it."

I do remember how much he enjoyed Halloween. For Senior Dress-up Day in high school, he went as the Jolly Green Giant. He dyed his hair and every inch of exposed skin green, and it took almost two weeks for the green to fade away completely.

John and Valerie had a heart-wrenching experience about mid-way through their three years in Okinawa.

> I had a miscarriage when I was over there, and that is the only time I've ever seen him be at a loss of what to do or say. They sent me home saying, "Yeah, you're gonna miscarry. Just go home and do it there." I never realized because I'd never had one, but it was excruciatingly painful. So much so, that I was almost . . . out of my body. He would ask, "What can I do? What can I do?" He felt helpless, and to see him helpless like that was painful itself. I remember I asked, "Can you make me a cup of hot tea?" and he said, "Ok," and started making it. Then I changed my mind and said, "No, I don't want tea." He poured out the tea and asked, "Ok,

156

what *do* you want?" and all I could say was, "I don't know what I want." He was (makes panic gestures) . . . he just couldn't do anything about it, and I can still see that look on his face. He was worried and scared to death for me but could do nothing to help. We ended up at the ER, and there was nothing he could do for me.

John felt enormous pain and frustration over not being able to do *anything* to help Valerie or to change the outcome. He wanted to be a daddy so badly.

A little over a year later as their three-year assignment was coming to an end, Valerie discovered she was pregnant again. They were cautiously excited but wanted to ensure the pregnancy was going well. "Back then, they wouldn't do an ultrasound, so we paid $50 and went off-base to make sure our baby was fine. So, I came home pregnant from Okinawa with Madison. She was our Okinawa baby."

16

Family Life—Good Friends

There is not a word yet for old friends who've just met.
~ Jim Henson

As military families deploy to the far reaches of the globe, they have to lean on each other for support. They start alone and end up with a newfound "family." John and Valerie immediately bonded with Mike West and his wife. Like John and Val, they had just gotten married and immediately moved to Okinawa. Mike and John already knew each other because their paths had merged at the end of the Combat Control pipeline. They were two of the seven to graduate from Combat Control School. Mike remembers,

> John and I first met on Lackland AFB at the OL-H INDOC the summer of 1989. He arrived a couple months after me and from what I remember about him, he was very serious and didn't say much (I would later learn that was definitely not him), maybe because of the level of physical activity demanded from all of us. Every day was a challenge and every

week the challenges became harder. We watched as multiple teammates did not pass the end of week evaluations, putting them at the mercy of the Air Force to select a new career field from vacancies that needed to be filled. John and Joe [Maynor] eventually settled into the class behind mine. Our class graduated that summer, and we were sent in different directions to multiple schools. As fate would have it, John and Joe joined us 6 months later in the [CCT] training pipeline at Air Traffic Control School, Keesler AFB in Mississippi.

At Keesler, we all quickly realized what kind of character John was. He shows up in this rusted-out Ford LTD (the size of a small tugboat) and I knew immediately that he would fit right into the mix. John and Joe were just as much a part of our team as anyone and, 6 months later, we found ourselves going through Combat Control School (CCS) together. From what I learned about John, we were a lot alike … loved vehicles, ladies, and being jokesters. After CCS, we headed in different directions once more, but our paths crossed again two years later when we arrived in Okinawa, Japan, at almost the same time for three-year tours.

Anyone who has been overseas on a military tour knows it has challenges and rewards. A major challenge is not having family support close by, so your military friends and teammates start filling those roles. Every holiday, birthday, special occasion and

… well, any excuse to have a barbecue … is with our military family. The best part is you really get to know each other and it's a very bonding experience. John's family and mine became the extended family for each other and, as I look back, it was priceless. We leaned on each other a lot and became really, really good friends.

Over the three years that John and Mike were stationed in Okinawa, they deepened their friendship, a kinship, by spending lots of time together. They had similar features which made them look like brothers, and they supported each other through everything . . . just like brothers. "It was to the point where trust was number one—where he could trust me and vice versa. We started to build that relationship; it was almost a competitive relationship like brothers. I really felt that and it was good; it was really good. We helped each other to the point where we felt like we could do anything and we were equals. Man, if one fell down, the other would help him get up."

Time on Okinawa was ending for John and Mike, and they found that their paths had so many parallels along the way. When the couples were leaving Okinawa, both headed to Pope AFB in Fayetteville, North Carolina, they discovered one more parallel. Mike's wife was pregnant too.

Back in the States and assigned to Pope, John and Mike marveled at the similarities of their lives. Mike says, "We were starting families at the same time. We got houses that weren't far from each other. We both checked each other's [houses] out and gave our thoughts and opinions about them, which was cool." John and Valerie's house was a cute three-bedroom ranch-style with a fenced-in backyard perfect for a growing family. Mike fondly remembers that time, "In 1996, I was there for Madison when she was born, and they turned around and came back to the hospital when my daughter was born just a few days later. We were starting lives together as fathers at the exact same time."

John and Val bought the house in Fayetteville and prepared for Madison's birth. Having suffered a miscarriage in Okinawa intensified the anticipation of their first little blessing, and when Madison was born, healthy and lively, they breathed a sigh of relief. She had John's intensely blue eyes and a head full of silky blonde hair. In her first year, Madison favored the Chapman side of the family, but as time passed, the Novak characteristics took over. She was a happy, inquisitive little girl, and John loved nothing more than being her daddy. He adored his tiny bundle of cuteness; she was his number one priority. John didn't balk at changing diapers, giving baths, feeding; you name it and he did it happily. But there *was* this one time . . .

Valerie instructed me to ask Mike about a certain "dirty diaper" incident. Mike laughed as he shared, "Shortly after our two girls were born, we ended up babysitting with each other. I think our wives had gone out together. Our job was to babysit. Of course, babysitting wasn't that easy because, you know, we'd end up doing something else outside or in the garage. The girls came back, and both Madison and my daughter Mikayla had smelly diapers. We had neglected our job as fathers because we were distracted by things out in the garage. It isn't like we were bad people, there were just . . . ten other things we'd rather be doing than changing a diaper. When our wives came in, they were like (makes "stank" face), 'What the . . . ?' So, maybe we neglected our part, but I think we ended up changing the diapers anyway." Men and their cars!

By the time Brianna came along two years later, John was an old hat at daddy duties; he just multiplied them times two. Blue-eyed Bri had a head of dark blonde hair that quickly grew into ringlets. She was a social little thing, wanting to be involved with whatever was going on. John loved playing with them, splashing in the tub as he gave them baths then lovingly brushing their wet hair, sitting on the floor and playing Barbies® with them, tossing them onto the couch or high into the air, or getting on all fours and letting them ride him like a pony. No matter what he did with his young daughters, they had his full attention. At home, his world revolved around them, including making things for them. Valerie remembers, "I had seen a crib at the store and I said, 'Oh, I want this crib.' He said, 'I could make that,' so we went to the store and he measured maybe three times. And then he made the crib. He could make anything." John also made their dressers, and many years after his death, Madison found his handprint on the inside of hers, left behind in wood stain. What a wonderful surprise. What a glorious gift.

Rachel and I visited when Brianna was around one, and we had such fun getting to know John's daughters. They used to call Bri "Brianna Banana" because she loved bananas. One morning, I awoke, went to the kitchen, and there she sat, wearing a diaper, a bib, and nothing more except banana smushed on her face. Her brilliant blue eyes sparkled over the shiny brown of the oxidized banana. John asked me what I'd like for breakfast, and she started slapping her open hands on the table. He shook his head and laughed as he said, "She always wants to join whoever is eating breakfast. She already ate with me and then the banana with Madison. Now she wants to eat with you." My mind's eye can still see her slapping those tiny hands on the banana-slimed table, and it makes me giggle.

Fatherhood was something John had always wanted, but it still surprised him how much he could love two little humans. He took his responsibilities very seriously as he began teaching life lessons at a level his sponges could understand. He instituted a sweet routine with Madison to teach the importance of telling the truth. Brianna wasn't quite old enough to completely understand the concept. If he asked young Madison, for example, if she had snuck some candy that was mysteriously missing, he allowed her to answer. He then made her pinky promise that she was telling the truth as he intertwined his big pinky with her tiny one and looked her in the eye. She was convinced that the moment their pinkies curled around each other he could see the truth, and she'd fess up to her transgression. Each time, John probably giggled inside, knowing the truth of the pinky promise, but was satisfied that he was building a solid foundation of life lessons.

Unfortunately, as in every life, not everything is giggles and fun. John told me a scary story about when Madison was three years old. He and Madison were in the driveway washing his vehicle, which was pulled nose-in toward the garage. He squatted at the front to wash the bumper, and Madison toddled around the vehicle, "helping" him wash when a funny feeling came over him. Still squatting, he leaned to peek around the corner and saw a car driving very slowly past the house. A man was at the wheel and a woman was in the passenger seat; both staring at blonde-haired, blue-eyed Madison. John stood up quickly, and as soon as the couple saw him, they sped off before he could see the license plate. He told me that story a few weeks after it happened, and even then, he was shaken and fuming. Like Mr. T used to say, "I pity the fool . . . "

Speaking of fools, John was center stage in a little gem Valerie shared. "We must have had a bad storm, and John was up in the attic. I don't know what he was doing up there, and I said, 'If you go up there, you're going to fall.' He said, 'I'm not going to fall through. Blah, blah, blah.' Well, guess what? I heard *thunk* from our bedroom, and there he was halfway through the ceiling. When he came down, he was soaking wet, and he was picking up all this stuff when he gave me this shitty-ass grin like, 'Ok. Yeah. Serves me right.'" This story made me laugh out loud. I can hear him cackling at himself. Smart ass.

Once John and Valerie had Madison and Brianna, the Harley-Davidson motorcycle felt unrealistic. They were riding it less often, and John had his sights set on a different vehicle. It all started with Mike West and a trip they took. Mike recalls,

> Shortly after we got to North Carolina, John and I went to a huge car show at the Charlotte Motor Speedway. It was a huge car sale, and one of the things that we saw was a little Cobra kit car made by Everett Morrison. When John saw it, he was like, "Man, I've always wanted to do this. This is it. This is the car I want to do," and I said, "Let's do it. What is holding us up?" We agreed to figure out a way to do it, so after we left the car show, I started looking and found a motor that was a perfect fit for a car like that; it would be a start. When I showed John, we agreed, "Let's do this," and we ended up getting a super rare motor at a great price. He sold his motorcycle, and we started building the car, buying up parts and pieces with this kit car. Once we got the motor, he started working on it and collecting parts while I started helping him assemble it. At the same time, I found another car for me that we bought in Raleigh. It was an old GTO, which, at the time, looked like a piece of shit, but John backed me up and said, "Man, I think this is something." I agreed, brought it home, and rebuilt it with his help. So, I had my GTO project, he had his Cobra project, and we supported each other. We had found common interests—going to car shows, hanging out, barbequing, and having a few beers. He always had Miller Lite® in his fridge.

I guess he sacrificed good beer to spend more on his car parts! After John died, Valerie had the difficult task of figuring out what to do with some of John's things, especially his beloved Cobra. Mike remembered,

> I was honored when Valerie and I talked about it after he died . . . there were only a few parts and pieces of the car that he had, and one of them was the engine we found together, the frame, and a few other parts that he started collecting. The cool thing was that she was moving it all to me so I could put it together. And I did. I assembled it from the frame, up. And, man, there's no doubt in my mind there was another guy helping me. When I got that car started for the first time, you don't . . . maybe for you, it's like when you hear the baby when it cries for the first time. When that engine started up, it was so cool. Having it means a lot to me . . . and there's not many people who have that effect on me. There are a few who are like family members; he was one. It's weird, in one of his boxes that I opened, there was his name tag, and it's in the car now. Chapman rides with me.

When Mike was talking about their cars, he remembered a story about the engine in his GTO.

> I rebuilt the motor, a lot of it was with his help, but I couldn't get it started. I had this car in my garage with a brand-new motor, and I couldn't get it started. When I got promoted, I had a pig barbeque. John was

there with another guy, Pat Elko, who was a friend I had met through John. They asked, "Hey, can we work on your car?" and I said, "Yeah, I'm hosting a bunch of people, so I'm too busy, but, man, I can't get this car started." So they're in my garage and, all of a sudden, I hear it fire up and the hair on the back of my neck stands up. "That's my car," and I went out there to find them smiling ear-to-ear, and John said, "We got it started. We figured out it was a wire." It's stuff like that, man. I'll cherish that for the rest of my life. That's when it's awesome when you've got a friend like that. He doesn't care about hanging out and trying to schmooze with people; he's out in the garage trying to help get my car started for the first time. Man, he got my car started. That was very important to me."

Pat also remembered when he and John got Mike's GTO started.

After some discussion and a few more beers, Chappy and I started messing around. Within about thirty minutes, we had the problem diagnosed and corrected. We started the GTO. It ran; it ran very well, and because it did not have any mufflers, it ran loud. Mike comes running out of the house with a complete look of disbelief. That look quickly turned to a huge smile. For years, every time Chappy and I would see Mike, he would talk about that day; the day we brought his pride and joy to life.

Pat met John in October of 1995. They went through the Operator Training Course at the 24 together and became fast friends. Toward the end of the course, they knew there would be a surprise trip to High Risk Survival School. In a letter Pat wrote to John's young daughters, he recounts a story from the survival school.

We knew this trip was coming, we just did not know exactly when. We had just come off a Close Air Support (CAS) training trip in Missouri. The team cadre said we were going to prepare for our final training exercise. We were going to conduct an assault on a compound back at Fort Bragg. We planned for the mission, packed our equipment, and loaded the plane.

While we were waiting on the ramp, one of the Base Operations airmen drove by. Chappy stopped him to ask if he knew where the plane was going. The Base Ops guy called someone on his radio, and in about a minute, we had the answer we knew was coming sooner or later—the survival school. Once we were in flight, our compasses all indicated we were heading west. If we were going to Fort Bragg, we should have had a heading east. This gave us time to contemplate what we would do. We were flying on a C-141. The load configuration for this flight had all of us sitting up in front with a pallet, our mission equipment, and three vehicles in the rear of the plane.

We eventually landed, taxied for a few minutes, and then the front crew door finally opened. The engines were still running, it was night, but we could clearly see that the people outside were wearing uniforms very different than those worn in the US military. Chappy and I decided to quickly make our way back to our rucksacks on the ramp. While in the back of the plane, hidden behind all of the vehicles, we could clearly see that the men in the funny uniforms were now in the front part of the aircraft, carrying rubber weapons pointed at everyone else, and sternly briefing the rest of our team. We watched for a few minutes, and Chappy decided to throw open the troop parachute drop door. We jumped out and ducked underneath the plane.

Had we run as soon as we exited, we would have been long gone; however, we hesitated. As soon as we realized they knew we were outside and were coming, we took off running. I remember one of our cadre, Butch McCumber, chasing after us. He was yelling, "You guys can run, but you'll have to come back through again." Apparently, the rule of the school was that the team instructors had to deliver us to the survival school instructors before they would be responsible for us. We looked at each other and decided to give up.

While Chappy and I were making our Great Escape, the rest of our team was getting briefed on the rules of the training scenario. For most of the training, we were kept in individual cells. They would pull us out every couple of hours to interrogate us. During one of the interrogations, they brought Chappy into the room with me apparently to pit us against each other. It did not work too well for us. Our stories did not match; we opened our mouths a little too often and took more of a beating than we probably should have. We did, however, steal the interrogator's sandwich when he left the room for a few minutes. We really had a good time with our petty theft even though we knew they were watching us.

Later on, back in our cells, they pulled [another guy] and myself out to let us eat some plain oatmeal on the floor area between the cells. I looked at [him] and said, "Let's jump the guard." He gave me that Homer Simpson look of complete ignorance, but he then said "Okay!" When the guard had us stand up, I dropped the hood they usually had us wearing over our heads. This young guard bent over right in front of me to pick it up for me. That is when I grabbed him. I was struggling with the guard, and I yelled to open the other cells.

Since John and Pat hadn't gotten the brief on the rules, Pat thought one of their responsibilities was to escape; it wasn't. If they didn't complete the school, they'd wash out and have to repeat it. So, when their team leader Captain Kurt Buller came out of his cell and saw what was happening, he called for an end to the escape attempt. He

171

gathered his men in a circle, linked arm-in-arm, said a few words, and sent them back to their cells to await the wrath of their "captors." They waited for two hours, expecting a harsh beating. Instead, they pulled John and Pat out of their cells and gave them the briefing everyone else had received while they were escaping on the runway.

I can't even imagine. They got beatings? John never divulged much about the training he went through to be a Combat Controller and then to earn a place in the elite squadron—The 24. I now understand how he could have stumbled along the way, but he never stopped trying. John made mistakes and had to find the will deep within himself to push on, but he did it. He succeeded where many others had failed. That is not a commentary on those who failed; it's just that John had the bit of extra grit needed to cross the finish line.

Before John sold his Harley to build the Cobra, and when he and Pat weren't enduring all kinds of unspeakable things in the name of training, they could be found riding around town together on their Harleys— Pat on his custom Sportster and John on his Softail Low-Rider. Pat included a story in his letter:

> We were sitting at a red light. Out of nowhere, when the light turned green, Chappy hit his throttle and took off like a bat out of hell. He was trying to pull a fast one on me, but I accelerated and passed him in just a couple of seconds. I guess he did not realize that even though my custom Sportster had less power and a smaller engine than his Low-Rider, mine also weighed almost 200 pounds less.

He was quite embarrassed after his little try at a race but was also impressed by how fast my little scooter really was.

That story makes me giggle. I can imagine him sitting there at the red light, machine rumbling under him, asking to be opened up. In his head, he gave one of his signature cackles and opened the throttle the second the light turned green. Almost instantly, his plan of smoking Pat backfired when the Sportster overtook and dusted *him*. I had a Sportster Iron a while back. I know what it can do. John could easily laugh at himself, and I bet he laughed heartily when he realized his mistake, most likely cackling out loud.

John, Valerie, and Pat became a little family of sorts when Pat started parking his Harley in their garage. His letter continued:

I really did not want to impose on Val and Chappy. Unfortunately, my scooter was slightly vandalized (at my apartment complex). That was the last straw for me. I remember when I first left it there; it was like a parent leaving their child to someone else's care for the very first time. This was the start of many, many nights for me at their home. They were kind of like my parents away from parents, except we would drink a lot of Miller Lite®. They fed me all of the time. I never went there with the intention of eating, but it seemed like they could whip up a feast in only a couple of minutes. John also let me know that he had to start my motorcycle every once in a while and ride it up and down the street to make sure it was okay. I am sure that was his intent (wink, wink). I think he probably did this a little more often after he sold his.

I bet he did. He loved his Harley.

Fellow CCT Bruce Dixon was someone John had met before, but he really got to know him once he arrived at the 24 on Pope AFB. Bruce thought about meeting John, "I came to the 24 in '97. I had met John before '97 because I was running a course he had come through, so I knew John; everybody knew John—Chappy as we called him. But I really got to know him when I went up to the 24."

Both John and Bruce had growing families that they preferred to spend time with when they weren't working. Neither partied with the single guys, at least not on a regular basis, and that commonality gave them something different to talk about when they were together. Bruce remembers,

> We didn't hang out that much. We'd talk about things they [the CCT] did in Okinawa, but when I got to know him, we actually talked about his girls. They don't know this, but we talked about some things that were going on with them. I remember, specifically, he told me how Madison was crying a lot and his technique was he'd just shut the door and let her cry until she got all the crying out. I

remember saying, "I'm not sure that's going to work with my wife and son" because we were having the same problem. But Chappy loved those girls, and he loved Val. You always saw his face light up when he talked about them. And as you know, I got to go out with them in Montana and spent ten days with them.

Bruce and David Gendron, another friend and CCT you'll meet later, mentored Madison and Brianna during a healing journey at the Legacy Project, part of The Station Foundation camp in Montana. The foundation is comprised of Special Operations community members and professionals who are dedicated to them. Their website states:

> The Legacy Project is a camp in which Gold Star children are given an opportunity to team up with warriors who served with and knew their parent well, giving them insight into their fallen warrior's life, and offering an opportunity to see their own personality traits as a reflection of that parent's heroic strength and commitment. The Legacy Project fosters self-confidence, preparing Gold Star children to cross the critical thresholds that lie ahead.[6]

When Bruce and David accompanied Madison and Brianna to the camp in July 2014, as designed, it offered

---

[6] "Legacy Project." The Station Foundation, 2011, https://thestationfoundation.org/.

healing for all of them. Bruce was Madison's mentor, and he shared some of his experiences.

I see Chappy in Madison; not physically, she looks like Val. Madison was the only one who caught a fish. We're going to fish and they're telling us what we needed to do, and I was supposed to stay with Madison and watch over her. She wants to go across to a little island in the middle [of the river] because she thinks that's where we're going to catch fish and I said, "Well, ok, I'm not going to tell you no; I'm supposed to go with you." The water must have been 40°, and she takes her shoes off. You're never supposed to take your shoes off, but she does so I take mine off, too, and we take off across. She makes it to the other side, and I split my pants. Because the water is so dang cold, I'm stopping and stopping. So, my shorts split and my Oakley® sunglasses fall and take off down the river and she says, "Come on, old man, what are you doing? Let's go."

Little things like that are what I remember. We did the first aid stuff together, and I could see she was confident; she would get the instructions, and she was confident just like Chappy. She'd hear it and would be able to do it. Bri was like that too. Both girls won the fire-starting competition, not because Dave and I helped them but because they paid attention when they were given instructions. It was a competition and, just like their dad and mom when it comes to competition, they smoked it.

Dave and I had a blast hanging out with them, getting to know them. We got to go on the honor hike, where we put rocks in our backpacks, and they picked the trail they wanted to take. The rocks represent the [emotional] load you're carrying; you're carrying all this stuff, and then they go up the trail. At any point along the trail, Bri and Maddie can pick out the area where they want to stack all the rocks up. In my opinion, they picked the best site because it's a place where the sun comes over the mountain and hits this little meadow. Dave and I got to talk a little bit about Chappy, and I took a team patch that I had from back in the day, put it there and stacked up all the rocks on top. All of the other Gold Star children and their mentors gave the girls hugs. It was a really cool and humbling event for me to be part of.

The men and women in the Special Tactics community have never stopped supporting our family even after all these years. They're an amazing bunch of people who set aside their own issues and pain to be there for any of us whenever the need arises. We're all pretty much settled this far out from John's death, but it's comforting to know guys like Mike, Pat, Bruce, and David are only a phone call away, as are so many others. Flipping the script on *To Kill a Mockingbird*, John proved that you *can* choose your family. His included not just his blood

177

relatives but so many from his career field. Not everyone became best friends with him, but he considered all of them family, and now they're our family too.

Steve "Nato" Coronato was another of John's Special Tactics family. He was a support guy—a radio man—at the 24. Like Mike and Pat, he also shared John's passion for cars.

> He could come down to the radio shop for five minutes to get a piece of kit, and he would walk away forty-five minutes later because we wound up talking about cars. He was building that kit Cobra, and it was like, "Oh man, I'm working on this, and I've got this problem," and we'd sit there and try to figure something out for him to do. "Hey, try this, try that." It was pretty interesting to chat with somebody about an interest of mine, as well, and how much he liked cars and the different TV shows about cars that we used to watch. We'd come into work and say, "Hey, did you see that episode of *Two Guys Garage* yesterday?"

Nato also shared his observations about John and his family. "So, we did two trips for training and then we had to do a three-month evaluation where we went to four or five different bases throughout that three-month timeframe. It took him away from the kids and Val for that whole time and he . . . you could always tell that

John missed them, he loved his little girls . . . at that time, little girls . . . " His voice dropped off as the memory from long ago tugged at him. Nato said that when the training stuff was done and they were able to talk about whatever, after starting with cars, the conversation always turned to his girls at home.

I never thought to ask John how he truly felt about being away from Valerie and their girls. Was he conflicted between the duties of his dream job and those of his little family? Honestly, I don't think there was a mental conflict until his final deployment. He had found the balance between work and home up to that point.

I asked Nato if he could sum up what John was like, and this is what he said.

> John was up at Virginia Beach on a TDY. We kept a lot of equipment there, and I had to go because John said, "Man, this place is just a mess. We don't have a handle on the equipment up in Virginia." I agreed, "Yeah, we need to have somebody come up here, do an inventory, check the things out." I was the lucky guy to go. I had never really been up in that area—hadn't really gone to where he was working before—but he took me right in, showed me around, got everything squared away. Even afterward, he said, "Come on over to the apartment and have a cookout." He was a good cook. It was a really good time. He knew how to take care of people. He was an Operator; I was a radio guy, a support guy; it's what I did for twenty years

with them. They broke the equipment; I fixed the equipment.

As a matter of fact, they didn't only fix equipment. Nato said that John and other operators sometimes went to him with an idea on how to modify or change some piece of radio equipment, and the radio guys would see if they could make it happen. Those guys could work magic.

Though Nato didn't say it, I had heard before that a small number of the type-A CCT didn't always treat support guys as equals. Those CCT weren't bad people; I understand that men who do what they do must have a certain personality to achieve at a high degree. John was different, and so many of his brothers have attested to it. He is not the only CCT to treat everyone with respect; most of them did, but there were some who didn't.

Like Nato, Billy Sasser was a support guy with the 24, except he was Life Support. He had nothing but praise for John.

Probably one of the most impactful conversations I ever had with John was when we were doing a jump trip, and we happened to be the last two guys on the packing mat. It's a big grass area where we pack the parachutes and jump in. We were just sitting there talking, and, you know, as a support guy in a unit like the 24, a lot of times, you're in awe of the things that these guys can do—just the vastly different skill sets that you've got to be good at to do your job. So, we were talking and he was telling me about some things, and at one point I told him,

"You know what? If I had known five, six, seven years ago about Combat Control, I would have loved to have tried to be one." And he looked at me and said, "You know what? I think you would have been a great Combat Controller."

In hindsight, I don't know if he really meant it, and that's not a bad thing, it's just that I think he felt at that point it was what I needed to hear, which showed a level of compassion and the connection he had with people. Like I said, it was probably what I needed to hear at the time because, you know, you can be in awe of guys, but at the same time, you have guys like John who were down to earth and would talk to you one-on-one. It didn't matter if he was a Combat Controller, and I was a Life Support guy; it was always person-to-person. That always stuck with me. And he would come down for no reason—not there to pick up something or do something. He would just swing by and sit there and a bunch of us sat around and talked and laughed.

I think, to a man, if you ask any support guy at the 24 during that timeframe, we'd all tell you the same thing. They could name a handful of guys who were that way. The great thing, too, is that because of my job in Life Support, we got the chance to do a lot of things with them. We'd do water ops, we were all HALO-qualified, so we'd jump, and when we went on a team trip, a lot of times they would include us. If you were having difficulties or struggling with something, John would always be the one to say, "Ok, do it this way, and it will be a lot easier, or try to do it this way," as opposed to some other guys would just laugh or start picking on you. In the 24, you have to have a very thick skin, but John was always, "Try it this way. Not that you're doing it wrong, you're jacked up, or anything like that but try it this way. It might be easier." And it was always constructive criticism and always very beneficial.

John didn't only help guys find easier or better ways of doing something, he was also protective of them. Billy shared another story that demonstrated John's protectiveness -- the same vigilance he had in high school. A group of Controllers, PJs, and support guys from the 24 were on a team trip somewhere in Nevada, and John not only helped Billy, but probably saved him from certain annihilation.

We were there for a week doing high-altitude oxygen jumps. The compound had a central building for the command center and the fire department, and then there were other trailers and buildings. The TV system had one controller in the fire department and whatever movie was being shown there was at every building—no individual channels. After a night jump, we were partaking in some frothy adult beverages, probably more than we needed, and I was in a building with several other guys. We went out and got some chicken. When we got back, porn was on the TV, and I don't like porn, so I called the fire department and said, "Change the porn. Put this movie on." I got a little resistance and *might* have called one, or five, more times before they changed it.

So, we're sitting on the couch, watching the movie, when *BOOM,* the door bursts in and it's the guys who were in the fire department. John was one of them. Harry [not his real name] was with him, and he said something to me, and I said something back. All of a sudden, he went from zero to nuclear—launched himself on me, got me in a chokehold. I had chicken in my mouth and, literally, I swear to God, to this day, when you talk about blacking out, you see it getting black like this (gestures disappearing eyesight), that's what was happening to me. The lights were going out. Then it suddenly stopped, and I was coughing up chicken and stuff. I turned around and John Chapman was between Harry and me, and he went off on him saying, "What the fuck are you doing? Mess with him again, you gotta go through me."

After that, they invited me to the fire station, and I didn't think about it until afterward, but Harry was sitting in one place and Chappy positioned himself between me and Harry. The next day, I thought two things: "Damn! I could have died last night." Then I thought about what Chappy did; he

183

acted on instinct. He saw somebody in trouble and immediately went to his aid. I thanked him the next day and said, "You know, I appreciate last night." He just said, "That's Harry." There were certain Controllers and PJs who were really highly thought of by the support guys, and Chappy was definitely one of them.

Billy's stories make me think about the benefit to treating everyone respectfully, no matter their rank or position. Who do you think would be more likely to get a special request filled by one of the support guys—someone who is a jerk to them or someone like John? I am in no way suggesting that's why John acted the way he did. His respectful treatment of others was natural and without thought of "what can this guy do for me?" But it's human nature to gravitate toward someone who treats you well, so the foregone conclusion is that if you are genuinely respectful, you might get bumped to the front of the line if you need help. Food for thought: Just be nice and, you may discover some freaking awesome people in the process like John did.

Another one of the "good guys" was CCT Mike Lamonica. He took a trip with John from Virginia Beach not long before he deployed to Afghanistan. Mike's memory of it may open a window into John's mindset at the time, but before I share it, I need to explain where John was at that time. Two-and-a-half years prior, he was trying to figure out what to do after retirement, which was only about 4 years off. He didn't want to work for any of the three-letter agencies like many guys do, wanting instead to be home more regularly for his family. John decided to move away from CCT and into the Survey shop at the 24. I'll explain more about that in a bit. Now, let's hear from Mike:

John had been on the Survey Team for about a year-and-a-half, maybe two. Your skills diminish very quickly, so he had to spin up very fast and go up and sit on Navy alert. At the time, I was aligned with the Navy, so I spent a lot of time coming and going and John was doing the same thing. We were just with different teams. I knew John was getting ready to depart [to Afghanistan], and that's when you guys had a death in the family; your grandmother. Basically, they said, "We need to get his replacement up there." I said, "Ok, I will drive him up and bring John back." We spent a lot of time in the bay just before they were ready to depart, and then John and I left.

The four-hour ride home with John was quite insightful for me. John and I didn't know each other really well, but I fully expected that drive to be about disappointment for not being with the guys and what was going on in Afghanistan, but we probably spent five minutes on that. The rest of the time he talked about his family and how taking this break to go and be with his family was the right thing. He also spent a lot of time talking about raising the girls with Val and the importance of that; the times that they had spent with friends

185

and how he enjoyed close friend relationships that helped raise the children as well. And he talked about a scenario where, when they were overseas, they would spend a lot of time where they lived—all the families would sit around and talk and hang out, and the kids could all run free. He enjoyed that aspect of the relationships around him, and he was very much a strong family man; it's what he talked about the entire time. He talked about what his aspirations were for the girls, and he and Valerie enjoying the time they got to spend together. He talked about riding the Harley a lot. They were all very intimate moments; stuff that I would have never known about John had I not spent those four hours with him. I didn't do a lot of talking; I really did a lot of listening. But John was very focused on getting home to spend time with his family. That's the last time I saw John.

I would argue that John's focus on family was forced upon him with our grandmother's death. It certainly made him switch gears from mentally preparing for Afghanistan to understanding that he needed to be with family. John was most likely torn over deploying with his team or going to Grandma's funeral. Ultimately, it wasn't his decision; his commander made the call, which took the burden of choice off John's shoulders. In my heart, I believe that if John had been given the final decision, he'd have opted to go with his team. Grandma was already gone, so he could do nothing about that, but he had been training with the team for months, and they were used to him. His loyalty and dedication to the team would have led him to Afghanistan with them. If the deployment had just been a training mission, he'd have opted for Grandma's funeral. But it *wasn't* training; it was war.

Hearing stories from John's military brothers amazed me how he could be a badass at work yet be so loving and gentle at home. There is a scene in the Kevin Costner film *A Field of Dreams* that I conjure whenever I think of him going home after training locally or after a TDY. In an extremely condensed version, Rookie Archie Graham is on the mystical baseball field created by Costner's character Ray. He had one at-bat in the ghostly game, something he never had in his real life, which occurred decades before. Ray's daughter fell off the bleachers next to the field, and they were about to call for an ambulance. Archie saw what was happening and ran to the edge of the field. He looked at his feet, the camera panning down the early 1900s baseball uniform to his dusty cleats at the edge of the dirt. He dropped his glove in the dust, and as he stepped off the magical field onto white pebbles, the cleats turned to men's dress shoes and his uniform transformed into suit pants. The camera pans back up his body to reveal Archie in his sunset years—Dr. Archibald "Moonlight" Graham, dressed in a suit and overcoat, carrying his doctor's bag. He walked to Ray's daughter and saved her life.

When I apply John to that scene, I see him approaching his front door dressed in BDUs (battle dress uniform) and carrying a heavy duffle bag. He stops with his hand on the doorknob and looks down at his combat boots. He drops the bag outside, and as he swings the door open and steps over the threshold, the boots morph into bare feet and the uniform falls away into shorts and a t-shirt. His little girls are waiting to play with him. John could leave the baggage of his job outside the house so that his focus on the inside was just being daddy.

How I wish he could have had more time being Madison and Brianna's playmate, mentor, teacher, and daddy.

PART THREE

CCT Graduate to Badass

Out of every one-hundred men, ten shouldn't even be there, eighty are just targets, nine are the real fighters, and we are lucky to have them, for they make the battle. Ah, but the one, one is a warrior and he will bring the others back.
~ Heraclitus

17

Brothers in Arms Remember

*Accept the challenges so that you can enjoy the
exhilaration of victory.*
~ George S. Patton

John never said much about what he did as an Air Force
Combat Controller. When someone asked me, "What
does John do?" I could only respond, "He's in Air Force
Special Forces," which isn't completely accurate, but
that's how I labeled it. The invariable response was,
"Air Force doesn't have special forces." I would shrug
and tell them, "Yeah, well, he's in it, so . . . " I had no
idea what it meant, and on the few occasions that I asked
John about it, he was always vague. Not long before he
deployed to Afghanistan, I asked him again what he did,
and he responded, "If you want to know what I do, read
Black Hawk Down" (by Mark Bowden). In it, Bowden
recounts the 1993 bloody battle of Mogadishu, Somalia,
and the heroes who emerged, some of whom were CCT.

John died before I could read it, and I still haven't. I
also used to love military movies but could not watch the
movie based on Bowden's book. Eventually, my husband

talked me into viewing it, and I think I cried through the entire film. Though I will watch military movies now on rare occasions, it is still difficult, and I have to be in the right frame of mind because my thoughts always go to John, no matter the timeframe or setting location.

A short dialogue that occurred during one of John's trips home demonstrates his attitude about himself and CCT. He and Kevin were with a few friends. Kevin shared, "We were out in public and the conversation had gotten around to what he did for a living. When John was asked, he simply stated that he was in the Air Force. When pressed further about what he did in the Air Force, his response was, 'Oh, I'm a chef.' Later when we were alone, I asked him, 'What's up with that chef thing?' His response was, 'I know who I am and what I'm capable of; I don't need to seek admiration from others.'" John's statement is the yardstick by which to measure who is truly a quiet professional.

Because John didn't reveal much about his career field, I must rely on those who trained and worked alongside him to tell that part of his story. Many of John's military brothers had difficulty remembering stories because so much time had passed, but there was also another issue. I was asking them to dig deep into their memories, but many, if not all, had suffered Traumatic Brain Injuries (TBI) at some point in their careers, probably multiple times. As one put it, "The TBIs hide or kill memories. Sometimes, if you tell us a story you've heard, it will jog our memories of something long forgotten; sometimes not."

There is a recurring sentiment among John's peers; one that each can validate with at least one story. To a man, John was regarded as quiet yet confident. He didn't feel the need to brag about his abilities; he demonstrated them with his actions. He was the same way in our childhood—on the soccer field, fixing a wrecked car, sticking up for underclassmen, or quietly being there for someone he didn't know. Childhood friend Brian Topor echoes what his teammates say, "John had no fear. He was quick-witted, bright, very smart. Confident; he wasn't arrogant, he wasn't reckless. He took risks, yes, but there's a difference between risky and reckless. He didn't fail."

It is clear this late in our virtual fireside chat that John would not have talked about himself had he survived, so I will let those who knew him well do it for him.

When he was going through Combat Control School (CCS) at Pope AFB, MSgt Ron Childress, Combat Controller and an instructor at the school, was a member of John's cadre. He and his wife Ann became great friends with John and Valerie, but before that, he put John and his fellow trainees through their paces. Ron remembers when he met John,

> I loved being an instructor, so I interacted with the students all the time. When I first met him, I kind of, you know, there's two kinds of students at Combat Control School—the real good ones or the real bad ones. John, I remember him because he was a little bit of both. He was a great student, but he was over-confident, and he had a right to be because he could back it up. But stuff came up.

> One day I was running the students through Camp McCall. They had all their gear on and everything,

193

and we ran the students down a sandy road and, all of a sudden, I hear *chink, chink, chink*. I stopped the formation, walked back, and picked up a magazine that was lying on the ground. I walked back up the formation and I said, "Whose magazine is this?" John Chapman says, "It's mine, Sergeant." I said, "What's the penalty for a dropped item?" and he says, "Ten four-counts." I said, "That's right," . . . *click, click, click, click, click* . . . "There's twenty-nine rounds in that magazine, so twenty-nine rounds and a magazine. How much is that, Chapman?" He says, "Three hundred four-counts." I said, "Start pushing North Carolina away," so, they got down and knocked 'em out. And the thing was, when they recovered after 300 pushups, 300 four-counts, he was still smiling about it.

Apparently, the passing of years did not reform John. Like the extra conditioning exacted on the soccer team because of his antics years ago, he and his fellow CCS students were "rewarded" with additional calisthenics thanks to John. I'm not saying he was goofing off, but ... I bet they were in really great shape!

Ron shared another story that not only gave him a nickname for John but also proved things hadn't changed since the day he was born.

As the field portion of Combat Control School went on, another day I told John, "Alright, ya'll need to get on the latrine for the bivouac site." He says, "Alright, Sergeant." So, about ten minutes later, he comes up to base camp where the instructors are and says, "Latrine's dug." I said, "You gotta be kidding me, Chapman." I went down there and looked and asked, "Where is it?"

Now, the latrine's supposed to be about six inches wide, four feet deep, and about six feet long; that's how it's supposed to be. I walked up and said, "Where's the latrine?" He said, "Right there." A little, bitty cat hole 'bout that big in the ground. I said, "Give me your hat." He pulled his hat off; I looked at it—seven and three-eighths. I said, "You got a big head, Chapman." I dropped it over that cat hole he dug and it was all the way over it.

From that point forward, while everybody else called John "Chappy," I called him "Big Head." For the rest of his life, I called him "Big Head Chapman," probably the only guy who did that. So anyway, after I figured out that little cat hole didn't meet Air Force latrine regulations, I found the gnarliest, rootiest tree and had him dig it out right beside that. He dug for about four hours on that latrine, getting through the roots, but it was good and quality standardized when he got through. And he smiled the whole time; he never got mad, he just kept digging.

Ron's story makes me wonder why John dug such a small whole in the first place. He *had* to have known what size the regulation latrine was supposed to be. Was he testing the instructors, daring them to punish him? All I can do is shake my head and chuckle.

★ ★ ★ ★

Jeremy "Scooby" Shoop was another of the seven men who graduated CCS with John. His story is different because he was part of a Kentucky team and joined John at the end of the pipeline.

As far as my interaction with Chappy, it was not long-term, but we went through Combat Control School together, so we got our berets together. My pipeline is sort of weird; so, CCS was my first meeting with him, and Chappy was one of three NCOs (noncommissioned officer) in our class. I was the officer, and then there were the three NCOs. Chappy was a buck sergeant at the time. The thing that stands out for me about Chappy, as far as the training that we went through, was that he had a gift. You're out there at Camp McCall or even on the Fort Bragg reservation and you're land naving (navigating); and whether you're on your own or in a group, a patrol file or whatever, there in North Carolina, you take a compass bearing, and you're looking at one pine tree amongst millions of pine trees that all look the same.

Your brother—it was uncanny—he could take a compass bearing, sight on a tree, and I'll be damned, he would not . . . it wasn't that he was focusing on that tree the whole time. No, but he would walk . . . to . . . that . . . tree. I'll tell you, the rest of us . . . your mind starts, you're sleep dep'd

196

(deprived), you're tired, you're hungry, you're hurting—physically hurting—blisters, abrasions all over you. Chappy, he'd take one bearing and would, I'll be damned, we're talking two- or three-thousand-meter legs through the woods, and he'd walk right to that tree. I'd ask, "How do you do that?" and Chappy would just say, "I don't know." That's the one thing I really remember about him. And of course, when we were combined into a full-sized patrol, you bet your ass I always said, "Chappy, you're compass man; you're map and compass man," because he just . . . land nav is a skill; it's an art. You let your mind wander for a few seconds in those woods and you're screwed; you lose your pace count, you're screwed. I don't think your brother was ever lost more than five or ten meters away from his calculations. It was uncanny.

So! While I get lost in parking lots *and* while using GPS (not kidding), John could navigate long distances, through thousands of trees, practically blindfolded! When was that skill developed? Maybe it started decades prior when Dad took the boys winter camping in thick woods. Maybe he always had a great internal compass. All I know is, I'm as impressed as Scooby!

After earning an assignment to the 24, John still kept in touch with his childhood friend Brian Topor. During part of his eulogy at John's funeral, Brian shared:

Upon being told by John that he completed training and became a member of the elite 24th Special Tactics Squadron, we were once again able to relive our dreams through him. At one point, John told me, "I get to train with Delta." Having grown up with an airport in our town, I said, "Delta Airlines?" John just looked at me and said, "Delta *Force,* you idiot." So, while John was not at liberty to share many details of the training or his assignments, what he did offer provided us with a sense of awe and overwhelming pride. I recall another conversation I had with John when he spoke of going to Texas for some training. When I asked him, "What kind of training?" John paused and then carefully responded, "Military training." It was then that I truly began to appreciate the level of training and nature of his duties and never again asked him to divulge what he was not willing or able to offer. I often hoped that, at some point well after his retirement, we would be able to have a few beers and coax more stories from John.

I bet a lot of people had the same thought; I know I did. John had two-and-a-half years until retirement when he was killed. That means we have missed out on over two decades of kicking back with cold beer and listening to stories that we now won't hear until we see him again in a much better place.

After almost two years at Pope, John was assigned his first subordinate; he was responsible for teaching the ins and outs of being on a CCT team. That man was Summa Stelly, a good ol' boy from Texas with a big heart and a southern accent that makes you have to listen closely. Like Shoop, Summa was with John briefly, but the time he did have left impressions and lessons that he still carries, long after separating from the Air Force.

A few days before he graduated CCS, Summa decided to check out his new assignment instead of going home like the others in his class. One of the first guys he came across was none other than MSgt Ron Childress. He introduced himself, "My name is Summa Stelly. I was hoping to find out what team I'm going to be on." Ron replied, "You're going to be on my Team. You're mine, boy. Now, you ain't met Chappy yet. He's a good man. He's in the team trailer. You go back there and ask for him. He's going to be your supervisor. You listen to that boy. He's a good troop."

Summa smiled at the memory of his first official meeting with John.

> As I'm walking up to the trailer, the door opens and Doug Thiel comes walking out with Chappy. I said, "Sgt Chapman, Summa Stelly." He says, "Hey, how are you doing? I just got told this morning I'm going to be your supervisor." I said, "Yeah, hope I don't embarrass both of us," and he immediately replied, "Oh, you're not going to embarrass us." He was standing there and had two brooms in his hand.

199

Now, I wasn't officially on duty, but I was in uniform. All my shit was tight; I had ironed my uniform, beret. I took about ten minutes just putting my beret on that morning. My first day at work, you know what I mean? And I had every intention of showing up and planning on overthrowing a government or some coup ... something really cool that you see in a James Bond movie. Chappy says, "Well, you're all dressed for work; come on, we're gonna start right now." And we go to this trailer, and he hands me a broom. We walked into the parachute locker, a single-wide trailer with a door on each side. He opens both doors and props them open. So, we go in there and Chappy says, "You see that room? We're going to be working in here today." We took everything out and set it in the parking lot. About an hour into it, I look at Chappy and said, "You know, I didn't picture my first day on the Combat Control team sweeping." He goes, "Did you have Sgt Rodman at OL-H?" I said I did and he said, "Well, Sgt Rodman taught you everything you need to know about being a teammate; you had it hammered into you. Now, you're going to learn how to shut your mouth and just do what you're told. Every day you come to work, you're starting over."

In the short time that I worked under Chappy, what was real cool is he took ownership in me. He had a unique perspective that I didn't have. Chappy spent time in the regular Air Force. I didn't. Being a CCT trainee was the only thing I knew. I had to learn how to be an operator. There's a big difference, and I really had to check my ego because I was a punk-ass kid like every other nineteen-year-old. Chappy kept reiterating, "Shut your mouth. Pay attention," and he would take time, real quiet in his way, teaching me about keeping my gear where I could see it all. He wouldn't criticize anybody but would say, "I want you to look in this locker. Can you work out of that?" One guy just had shit everywhere and he goes, "You're not helping yourself, and you're not showing this team any respect. You keep your shit stacked away." I'd look at his locker. It was organized. It would be used, but everything had a place. And it wore off; I kept my gear almost identical to what he showed me. I'll never forget how Chappy took ownership of me and, at no point, was it not conscious in my mind that the things I did were a reflection on the guy who trained me.

Summa only had a few training missions with him before John left for Okinawa in 1992, but he remembers them like they were yesterday. On one trip, they were going to do their six-month surface and night swims. He said, "We were on this dive trip on Wrightsville Beach, and we had to do a surface swim. It was three days of hard work and long swims; you have to do a day swim and a night swim. The first day, we did it daytime, and then the first night we did our surface swim because it's usually the hardest. It's a kickass drill and you want to do it first."

What was supposed to be an hour-long swim turned into three and a half hours due to five-foot sea swells and a thirty-degree drop in temperature. Summa remembers, "We only brought the shorties—the wetsuits with the top and your legs had no wetsuits on them. Visibility was good, it was just dark. But the current coming out was nasty." There was talk of postponing the swim, but John offered up the first vote of, "Let's just get this done," and the rest followed suit although some would have preferred to try the next day. Once the challenge was out there, no one wanted to be the "sissy." After the swim, they dragged themselves onto the shore, exhausted but glad it was over and done.

Summa thought about it further and continued,

> Chappy showed me how to set the tone for anything I did on the team. He gave me his insight every time. He was also real conscious about . . . they called us "new breed," the guys that went through OL-H. Well before OL-H, it wasn't mandatory that Combat Controllers were SCUBA-qualified. There are some guys who were not good swimmers. They were good operators, well-respected guys but water wasn't their strong suit. It wasn't mandatory when they went through. But he was real conscious about it. He told me, "Look, these older guys, you'll learn from them, but they're not as proficient in the water as you are. It's real important that you don't show them disrespect. It's important that you give them dignity; it wasn't mandatory when they signed up. And you give them the dignity of not disrespecting them."

I nodded my head in affirmation at everything Summa said about John. The man he knew was the same little boy I grew up with; the same young man who exhibited understanding, compassion, and duty in high school. I see his team mentality; I hear the deep respect he held for so many. It's why he impacted so many lives. It's why so many respected him. Time and "life" never changed who he was.

Summa also shared a couple of stories that expose John's "little rascal" side. It's no surprise that some things never changed!

> I got to thinking about the last time I talked to Chappy. I remember the last time I spoke to him he was in Kadena [Okinawa, Japan]. I was working a drop late that night, and he was calling to leave a message for admin. He told the guy working CQ [Charge of Quarters, the one who guards the front entrance to barracks or other buildings], "Tell Stelly to call me at this number." So, when I got back from working my drop, I called him and he asked, "Thought about where you're going?" I had already put my package in to reenlist. I was working the next night, and Cliff Blair said, "Stelly, there's a fax that came in for you." I went to go look at it, and it was a Xerox® copy of Chappy's ass.

According to Summa, and I completely believe him, copying his rear end was something John liked to do, either as a joke or a visual "kiss my ass" to the recipient. I imagine he often cackled to himself as he was doing it. Before John left for Kadena, Summa witnessed a comical butt-copying event.

> So, we got back that night [from a trip] and were unloading our gear. We come into the squadron and Cliff says, "Hey, I gotta run this to Intel; will y'all watch the phones for me?" When the door shuts, Chappy says, "Hey, sit your ass by the phone. I gotta take care of something." There was nobody in the squadron. It was the end of the day, so everyone was gone. Chappy noticed this brand spanking new copy machine; it was high-speed— nicest they made. It would copy, fax, do all of it in one. This was cutting edge. Chappy had this look on his face. He had this thing about Xeroxing his ass. He had this plan; he was going to write this SOP [standard operating procedure] . . . a checklist . . . *The Proper Way to Make a Xerox® Copy of Your Ass*. He had this whole thing; it was like a joke, but he was serious. He had a checklist, how you're going to break it down, whether you liked the person, whether you wanted to do it operations security, whether you wanted to do it without them knowing it was from you, or if you wanted to send some kind of signature. It was funny how he could write it down.

> So Chappy goes, "You call if Cliff comes back." I didn't know what was going on. This copy machine is still in the box, still had Styrofoam, it was wrapped up. He started ripping it open. He

finds the cord, plugs it in, finds a telephone cord and plugs it into the back. It comes alive and he says, "This is awesome." He pulls a chair up to it, gets on the chair, and drops trou. He picks the lid up, and he played with it a couple of times because it was the kind that the top didn't move; it had something inside that just scanned. I asked, "What are you doing?" and he says, "It's a need-to-know basis. Get your ass in there. You need plausible deniability; you can't watch." So, I go back in the other room and I hear *BOOM*, like glass breaking. I stick my head in, and he's climbing off of it. His eyes are about that big around. He sat on it, busted the glass, and fell through it. He closed that thing up, threw the Styrofoam back in the box, pulled the box up there and got some hundred-mile-an-hour tape and taped the box back and said, "We're out of here." In the parking lot, we hugged it out and said, "Keep your powder dry," and that's the last time I put my eyeballs on him.

I nearly peed my pants as Summa shared that story and I laugh every time I reread it. I can see the whole event unfold and John's shocked look when his little plan went terribly off the rails. I had seen that expression many times, the earliest of which might have been the "poop" incident when he was eight. Did whoever opened the "new" copier figure out who busted it? If not . . . "now you know."

205

I couldn't write about John without including thoughts and stories from friends and Combat Controllers Bruce Dixon and David Gendron. I'll start with Bruce. Our family met him for the first time at John's funeral. We probably met him at the memorial service on Pope, but none of us remembers much about that day; the loss and pain were too recent and raw. One of the things I *do* remember from that time was how much Bruce resembled John. I'm pretty sure we ended up making him a little uncomfortable when Mom or I asked him for a "Johnny hug," but he was so kind; he always provided a much-needed embrace.

The first night in town before the wake and funeral, a bunch of family and friends met John's squadron brothers in the bar of a hotel. We drank the bar dry, but it was time together we all needed. While telling stories around the tables, one CCT told us about coin checks—how team members tried to have a challenge coin on them at all times in case someone yelled, "Coin check!" If everyone present has a coin, the challenger has to buy a round of drinks. If someone doesn't have a coin when challenged, drinks are on that person. And if someone drops a coin by accident, drinks are on him. Someone told us about a time when John was in the shower, buck naked, and someone yelled, "Coin check!" John didn't buy drinks that night. I'll let you imagine where he had his coin. And one time while Scuba diving, someone invoked the coin check demand deep under water. Nope! Not this time, either. John's coin was in his mask.

At the wake the following day, Bruce was coming through the line with his fellow 24 guys when he stopped to talk with me. I immediately said, "Button check." Poor Bruce didn't have a clue what I was talking about. I asked, "How could you not know?" After talking it out, I realized that *I* was the one who didn't have a clue. He laughed with me and ended up giving me a special coin that he was going to leave on John's casket the next day. It remains a treasure of mine. (I still laugh at myself over that; "Button check," what was I thinking?)

Bruce smiled as he remembered a time at Pope AFB when they had an unannounced "Monster Mash" (a Special Tactics fitness competition) that included all sorts of physically and mentally challenging events.

> Some of us had caught wind about the monster mash, but I don't know that Chappy knew it was going to happen. Chappy was one of those guys who, "Don't mess with my time. I don't like organized PT; I'm an operator, and I do what you ask me to do, but it's my time." So, he didn't particularly like the mash. We had an event at the Army pool, and their diving board is Olympic-style; it's over twenty feet high. Chappy and I were encouraging others who didn't quite like the height to just go. After we were all done, he got up on the edge [of the diving board], and we thought he was just joking around because he's spreading his arms out and he's got his toes on the edge, and I'm like, "Let's go, Chappy, we gotta go." And he does this dive, and I don't remember what it was—it was probably like a two-and-a-half gainer or something. It was an inward dive, and we all said, "Holy crap!" Others knew he was a good

diver, but not *that* good. But he never . . . that's the kind of guy Chappy was . . . he didn't tell you. He didn't go around bragging about how good he was at anything; he let his actions show how good he was at stuff. Now, he would give you a hard time and would joke; he had a lot of wit. He was witty, so you didn't want to get in a wit match with Chappy, but I just remember thinking, "Man, I had no idea." There are some guys who say, "I played football. I was the quarterback. I almost made it to . . . whatever." Chappy's not that type of guy.

As I listened to many of John's CCT brothers, I discovered he didn't only have *their* respect, but he also earned it from others. Bruce shared a little about that.

He was talented and the organizations we worked for, elite organizations, had such respect for Chappy. Like when you go into a room for a meeting, and you're going to talk about the exercise you're gonna do and all the guys . . . you just see the respect and the bona fides that he has when he walks into the room. And it was impressive because just being associated with Chappy, they say, "Oh, he's with Chappy, then he knows what he's doing. They've got it under control." That was one of the things I noticed right away.

While discussing John and the book, someone from outside the CCT community suggested that I be careful about portraying him as always being a good guy, and I get it; I truly do. People like to see challenges, triumphs, and a bit—or a lot—of failure. Taking that suggestion to heart, I asked Bruce if he had ever witnessed a time when John wasn't on his game or was struggling with something. Bruce shook his head before I completed the question:

As operators, we all pride ourselves on being competent, and he was. He was one of those guys who could go into any situation, any training event or real-world situation, and he always knew his stuff. You would never hear Chappy say, "Hold on, let me read up on that and then I'll be ready." He was *always* ready. And Chappy had confidence in everything he did as an operator. Even beyond that, he was just a confident guy. Like I said, when he walked into the room, whether he was a formal leader, he was always an informal leader behind the scenes. Ready. The one thing we pride ourselves on, especially in that unit, is to be ready. You could judge a guy by how he kept his cage, and his gear was always ready; he was always ready to go at a moment's notice. And he was trustworthy. I felt like I could go to Chappy and talk to him about anything and he did give you a hard time, especially if something was funny; he would make fun of you but in a good way that didn't set you off. But then he would help me.

I spoke with Bruce for quite some time about John and he kept going back to the type of person John was. The respect he has for John was evident as he spoke.

I talked about being trustworthy and being confident and the confidence he always had. The one thing I would say also is his bravery because I watched Chappy in training events where other guys were kinda like, "Let's step back; let's take a look at this, it looks pretty dangerous," and Chappy, I never saw fear in his eyes. I'm sure, inside, there was probably fear, but I never saw it. Looking at video [the drone/AC130 video of the battle on Takur Ghar] of his heroics on that mountain; that's beyond brave. We're all brave to do what we do, but what Chappy did on that mountain was the stuff that Medal of Honor recipients are made of. People have said Chappy wasn't in the best shape. Holy cow, you look at how high he was, the elevation [10,469 feet], and he *charged* that machine gun nest, the enemy. When everybody else was hunkering down, he charged, and it was in two feet of snow. You could see how fast he moved out, so it wasn't about . . . Chappy didn't need to go out and run ten miles to show you he was in shape; right there [on the mountain], it was all heart. "I'm going to take care of my team. My teammates are getting shot at, and I'm going to engage the enemy and make sure they're safe." That's what Chappy was all about.

Bruce's words resonated with me. He was describing the boy I grew up with; the brother who told Tammy he would do whatever it took to protect his team. I asked if he would delve a little bit into when he heard John had been killed. It's never an easy subject, but he was willing to share.

When Chappy was killed, we were going through training about two weeks before I was supposed to go over [to Afghanistan]. I remember going into the hotel room, and we were told, "John Chapman's been killed in action," and it was like a punch in the gut for all of us. I mean, really, and it was two weeks before a lot of us were going over. And I'll tell you what it did to my family too. At that point, my kids thought their dad was kinda invincible—like a cartoon character. They watch Saturday cartoons, and the guy falls off a cliff and bounces right back up. That's kinda how they looked at us but then, they knew John, they knew the girls. So now, especially the youngest at the time, Cody, could see, "I knew him, now he's gone and my dad's going in two weeks." It was very, very hard. After that, when I left two weeks after Chappy was killed, Cody held onto me; he had never done that before. He screamed, "Do not leave. Do not leave." It was the hardest thing I had to do.

Thank you, Bruce, for sharing such a personal and emotional story. America needs to know the toll deployments have on our military families, especially the youngsters. Pair the separation with hearing of deaths or injuries and just imagine what *that* does to them. I've said it many times before, and I'll say it again: Thank you to all service men and women for what you do, no matter your location, rank, or career field. Without you, I shudder to think where this country would be, and

Bruce's story shines light on just a small part of what our military families endure. Thank you to the families too. You support and endure quietly so our warriors can do what they do.

Dave Gendron, the CCT who was Brianna's mentor at the Legacy Project in Montana, slowly became friends with John through training operations, squadron meetings, and social functions even though they weren't always on the same team. He sent me an email that took time and emotion to complete, and I will share some of it. Be prepared, Dave has quite a knack for writing and should be a writer himself.

Before moving into the meat of the email, Dave started with his heart.

> The first thing I'd like to say is how incredibly privileged I feel to have known John. I can't recall the first moment he and I met, but I imagine that's the nature of our business. Guys would show up for the team, and we wouldn't offer much in the way of friendship and camaraderie until they were selected to operate on one of the teams. "Street cred" only went so far; even internally, one had to prove himself. I don't think it took your brother very long to do just that. Though there are many stories of bars and beers, those can be told about any number of fellow CCT. Below are words that I can share about only one—John Chapman.

When John and Dave first met, they were on different teams but, "we trained together on jump trips, shooting schools, comms [communication] training, and even dropped a few bombs (inert) out on the Ft. Bragg range. Being on different teams meant a bit of intra-team rivalry, but he and I never got too caught up in all of that."

One of the best stories Dave shared with me puts John's commitment to the team on full display while Dave's colorful prose turns an otherwise unremarkable event into a CCT sitcom.

Chappy was tasked with supporting our Army counterparts during a training exercise in Florida. He was to be attached to the recce [reconnaissance] element, and I was a nug working in the Tactical Operations Center (TOC). The op was to infiltrate a MOUT (Military Operations in Urban Terrain) site, seize the cargo, and kill or capture bad guys. It was a fairly routine exercise. John was to move by vehicle to a drop-off point and then move overland, by foot, to the objective.

As Chappy planned, packed, and prepared for the op, I twiddled my thumbs, reviewed notional intel, and pretty much sat on my ass. As day turned to night and final preparations were made, guess who comes strolling into the TOC, looking like a bag of smashed ass? Yup, ole Chappy! Eyes watering, snot running down his upper lip, "GN, I'm out." [GN is Dave's CCT Operating Initials.] I thought, "Ok, no CCT with recce." I contacted the squadron and was met with the suggestion that I fill in. "WTF?" I didn't even support that squadron when I was operating. I knew no one on the recce element, and I had no operational gear of my own. I walked back to Chappy pissed, of course, and read him in on what was going on. We had a few hours until launch, and he was prepping me with frequencies, call signs, execution checklist calls, infil routes, exfil procedures, and introducing me to the guys I'd be rolling with. I was so pissed! I had to jump through my ass, and he was gonna spend the night sleepy-sleepy in a cozy hotel room.

I got as prepared as I could while Chappy changed out of his BDUs. Oh, yeah, I'd be wearing his kit. I'm 6'2" and Chappy was 5'10" in heels! "This should be good," I thought. I slipped into his uniform and couldn't help but feel like an ass. I damned sure didn't have to worry about blousing my trousers; they hung about four inches above my ankles! I looked like Pee Wee Herman. Insult to injury, I didn't have gloves long enough to cover my exposed wrists due to the child-length sleeves on his shirt! By the time I was dressed (in a boonie hat half a size too big, Pee Wee's pants, lollipop guild shirt, and my freshly polished garrison boots), I looked like some wanna-be heading out for his first paintball shoot in his little brother's gear. Had he not felt like shit, I'm sure Chappy would have laughed his ass off.

There I was, driving across Florida to a hit I knew nothing about, with elite warriors I did not know, unfamiliar kit, and all because Chappy had the sniffles. I'd like to say everything went off without a hitch, but you know, Murphy's Law! Our team reached the objective rally point, I set up the radio and started passing info back to the TOC. The recce team leader gave the op a go and the assault force moved in. We were about to link up with the assault squadron when we heard the "medic up" call. A breacher was seriously injured by a premature blast of one of the door charges. Now I'm scrambling to find the freq, call sign, and execution checklist call for requesting a med-evac. It's hot as shit, bugs are eating me alive, and worst of all, we've got a man down. So, there I am, in my clown suit, team guys running around everywhere, squadron SGM yelling in my ear, helos overhead, TOC on the radio, and all I can think about is kicking Chappy's ass out of that comfy bed and taking a dump in it! The rest of the mission was scrubbed, and we departed the training area. The whole ride back to the TOC, I'm cursing Chappy and fighting mad.

It was probably 0300 or 0400 when we pulled up to the TOC. The SGM, Major, and troop leadership moved inside for the debrief. I secured Chappy's gear and moved inside. Still steaming, I looked toward what should have been my empty seat at the comms table. There was Chappy! He hadn't gone back to the hotel . . . not for one minute. He was in his PT gear doing my job. I wondered if anyone around me could see how much of an ass I felt like. Chappy was up all night, snotty, watery-eyed, and miserable along with the rest of us. John Chapman earned his stripes that night, with me anyway. We never mentioned a word of it to each other, ever. I wonder what he'd say to me today.

I'd be willing to bet that John would first confirm he definitely would have laughed his ass off had he not felt so poorly, and then he would thank Dave for stepping in even though it was the last thing he wanted to do that night. After that, he'd make fun of Dave again, erupting in his signature cackle, and describing the scene as *he* had witnessed it. This story is "only" about training; can you imagine the stepping up that happens in real-world situations? I can. John stepped up big-time on the last day of his life.

As Dave continued his email, part of another story parallels Bruce's memory of how John was always prepared, always ready. Even though I grew up with him, it surprised me a little because, back in the day, aside from our battles of wit, John did not seem to be the cerebral type. He was an average student, achieving As and Bs in grammar school, but when he got to high school, he pulled mostly Cs. I discovered just how far above average he was when two of his CCT brothers made comments to me. Bart Decker (yes, *that* Bart Decker, the first airman to step foot in Afghanistan after the terror attacks of 9/11, and one of the twenty-first-century horse soldiers depicted in *12 Strong*) shared the following.

> [An instructor] said he never wanted John to ask a question because he always already knew the answer. Maybe he asked questions for the edification of others in the room if he already knew the answer; either that or he wanted to put the instructor on the spot.

Mike West also witnessed John's intellect, "We were in a class with a new instructor who was trying to teach out of a manual. It was high-level math and he was struggling. John stood up and said, 'No, you've got that all wrong,' and he proceeded to teach the class himself."

High-level math?! It shouldn't have surprised me, but it sure as hell did. It also explained a few things, like how he was so good at marksmanship and land navigation, among so many other things. John's brain functioned on a level much higher than I ever knew. I joke about it sometimes and say, "He hid it well. Haha!" These two little stories confirmed what his grades failed to reflect: John was a very smart guy, and perhaps *he* was actually the deepest thinker of the four of us kids.

After Dave confirmed John's preparedness, the rest is a comedic example of what our warriors sometimes face.

> Around the summer of '99, Chappy and I found ourselves working together in the 24's Integrated Survey Program. Chappy had beaten me there and was already an experienced surveyor upon my arrival. Our job with the Survey Team took us into a more tech-savvy world, laser range finders,

computers, and digital cameras. Instead of briefing aircrews and grunts, we were now advising [high-level people]. We travelled all over the world to assess diplomatic facilities.

When I showed up, the only desk left was right next to [John]. He was quick with a welcome but got right down to business; he was going to be my trainer. I was none-too-happy about being on the team, and Chappy bore the brunt of my sarcastic behavior. I was no computer geek, but he made quick work of explaining things down to my level. Our first survey trip was coming soon, and he was hell-bent on making sure I was fully capable before departing.

The day finally came to take our first survey trip together. We would make the day-and-a-half journey to breathtaking (insert sarcasm) Monrovia, Liberia. Given Uncle Sam's propensity to save money only at the lowest levels of government, the cheapest flight was booked through somewhere in Europe. That's right! Fly to Europe to get to West Africa.

I'm not sure if Chappy was some sort of self-proclaimed history buff, but for the first eight hours of our trip, I learned more about Liberia than anyone has a desire to know! "Dude, Liberia was founded, established, colonized, and controlled (by the US) as a colony for former African American slaves and their free black descendants." And so it went until I wanted to jab both of my ears with a dull, rusty ice pick. More than once I asked, "Where the hell do you get this shit?" After all, there was no Wikipedia yet. He'd hit me with a wry smile and push his face back into his *Road and Track* magazine. I'm pretty sure world history is NOT a major topic in *R and T*!

We arrived at our European stop in late morning and had a four- to five-hour layover. This is the time you really start needing a shower or your teeth brushed. You're cranky and want to crawl under a moving bus just to get away from the hundreds of strange travel mates. Luckily, when we were called to board the final leg of our trip, I discovered that I'd be sitting with a farting, belching, and storytelling friend. John was my seatmate.

As we crossed the tarmac toward the plane, the reality of what we were about to travel on came into clear focus. An early 80s Harbin Y-12! At the time, it wasn't all that old, but that horse was "rode hard and put up wet." The closer we got the more I wanted to turn around and get back to the terminal with 500 perfect strangers. The paint was faded, peeling, and seemingly applied by brush. The right-side tire was three-quarters flat and the starboard engine had a #10 can hanging on a metal wire beneath it to catch leaking oil. As the rear door swung open and the stairs dropped to the ground,

Chappy turned to me, and after a short pause, both of us broke out in gut-wrenching laughter. We were the first to board and were greeted by one of the hardest-looking men I'd ever seen. He waved in the direction of the seats, and with a deep, raspy growl, uttered, "Velcome on bort.' This should be interesting.

We took our seats—me at the window and Chappy on the aisle. He fastened his belt as I quickly realized two things. The seat was nothing more than a steel pan covered with blue and grey seat covers with zero padding. The second was that I was gifted with two male ends to the belt. Always looking out for his best buddy, Chappy calmly and quietly said, "Just tie the two together," and proceeded to reach over to assist. "No thanks, brother! I got this." We chuckled.

As decrepit as the outside looked, the inside was worse. The plastic that lined the inside of the fuselage was virtually all removed, none of the lights worked, and the first two rows of seats were missing because they needed room for the goats and chickens, of course. The smell was awful and got worse when the doors were closed and we proceeded to taxi. It was like riding in a dump truck on a gravel road. We didn't speak much on the flight—not because there was a lack of conversation material; we just couldn't hear a damned thing. Even with earplugs and headphones, it was the loudest plane we'd ever been in . . . ever!!

The end of this story is a bit anti-climactic. We landed safely and went about our business; however, every minute leading up to that trip with Chappy will stay with me forever. We never traveled together again, but I have been involved in that program ever since, and I still use many of the lessons taught to me by a good teammate and better friend. I owe him more than I could ever repay.[7]

John wouldn't have seen it that way. Dave owed him nothing but the wonderful friendship they had. After John was killed and his body arrived at Dover AFB to be prepared for burial, the unit needed two men to escort him to the funeral home in Windber, Pennsylvania. It was originally going to be two officers, but First Sergeant Longfritz insisted the roles be filled by "two of the guys," so, as he and Dave stood tearing up outside of John and Valerie's home, he asked Dave to be one of them. He immediately accepted and offered that Scott Toner should be the second escort. I cannot imagine how difficult it is to set aside your own grief to stand guard over your fallen brother without showing your pain. I get emotional thinking about what they did for my brother and theirs. Thank you, Dave and Scott.

---

[7] For brevity and my concerns about sharing too much, I have edited and/or omitted some of what David shared. I know he'll understand.

On a much lighter note, and one I guarantee John would fully appreciate, Dave shared one more tidbit: "My most vivid memory of our days training in the team room has nothing to do with any story but is worth the share. The med [medical] shop was right across the hall and each of us (mostly Chappy) made it our daily mission to stink up the joint. I'd swear on a stack of Bibles that dude ate beans and cabbage every single day; he was rotten."

Yes, yes he was.

I couldn't leave my husband out of this chapter. He was John's First Sergeant long before he became my spouse, so he has seen both sides of losing someone to war. Kenny was nearing the end of his Air Force career when John was killed, but he hadn't been ready to pull the plug until the awful news hit him. As he said, "When Chappy died, it just wasn't fun anymore, and I knew it was time to retire." He had gone with Col Ken Rodriguez to notify Valerie, and he never wanted to have to do that again. He knew the pain of losing a troop, a brother in arms. After marrying me, he also discovered the pain of losing a blood brother and has lived that loss from a sister's perspective too. Kenny is quick to say he didn't know John extremely well during their time together at the 24. As First Sergeant, he wasn't usually invited to weekend barbeques for various official reasons. And even if he *had* been invited, John probably wouldn't have been there. When he wasn't working, his priority was Valerie and their girls. Kenny said, "It makes me sad that I didn't get to know John well when we worked together. There just weren't many times that we needed to interact. I'm getting to know him so much better now after he's been gone. I wish things had been different; he's someone I'd have loved to hang out with." I think John and Kenny would have quickly become more like brothers than brothers-in-law. We are blessed to have each other now; we just wish he was still with us too. John fulfilled his promise to me from years before: he brought Kenny and me together. As sad as the start of our relationship is, he would want our story to be shared. Good *can* come from tragedy.

These stories from John's CCT days attest to his complex character—thoughtful about some things, hard-headed about others, and never losing his mischievous side. He also had a bit of defiance in him, seeing how far he could push limits and sometimes out-and-out breaking the rules. John was brazen enough to find out if and how far they could be bent or broken. Mike Lamonica shared a story, which beautifully portrays his audacity. It happened a few years into his CCT career.

> John had a bit of a defiant side to him. We were going into a training area, and they briefed us. They said, "Tomorrow we're all going to meet here; be here at this time, and you're not allowed to bring your personal vehicle." John and I were riding together, so he said, "Hey, meet me here and I'll

pick you up." So, he picks me up in his Jeep. I'm like, "Hey, we're not supposed to be doing this." The instructor is, we'll say, not the nicest guy; John and he didn't get along. John basically said, "Yeah, I'm doing this out of spite. I want to see him punish me for this." It was funny because John's his own man. He didn't follow the path of least resistance; he didn't do what people told him just because they told him, and sometimes he would do things the opposite as well. It's another thing I liked about the guys we worked with; they made very measured decisions. They'd go, "Hey, here's the risk of my decision, but I'm willing to accept it." It wasn't a real big deal; the instructor never really noticed, and nobody ever said anything, so in John's mind, he got a victory and he laughed about that.

I am *sure* it was his cackle laugh.

This chapter is titled "Brothers in Arms Remember," but I think it's the perfect place to share Kevin's final message to them during his Hurlburt speech.

John is my brother, but he's also your brother, your brother in arms, and as I get to know each and every one of you, I can feel you becoming my brothers and sisters as well. To my brothers and sisters in the legacy of John, as I hear your stories of John, I hear how his humility has impacted all of you as well. From Proverbs 11:2 we learn, "When pride comes, then comes disgrace. But with humility comes wisdom." For John, humility was second nature because his esteem was always focused on others instead of himself. He had the innate ability to see the big picture in any situation, which gave him the wisdom to take command and control of the environment in which he found himself.

John 3:16 says, "For God so loved the world that he gave his only begotten son that whoever believes in him should not perish but have everlasting life." Jesus willingly sacrificed himself for the salvation of the world. Jesus commands us to love greatly in John 15:12-13, "This is my commandment that you love one another as I have loved you. Greater love has no one than this than to lay down one's life for his friends." The act of laying down your life for your friends can only come from one who embodies humility; one who considers others before he considers himself. And finally, I come back to 1 John 3:16, "By this we know love because he has laid down his life for us, we ought to lay down our lives for our brethren."

On a cold morning on the fourth of March in the year 2002, in a place called Takur Ghar, John undertook his final act of humility. Hearing the approach of his rescue helicopter, he assessed the situation and made a command decision. That decision esteemed his rescuers more than himself. This final act was the ultimate expression of his love—his love for his brothers, his love for his country, his love for me, and his love for all of you.

Well said, my dear brother. Well said.

18

Officer Brothers in Arms Remember

The characteristic of a well-bred man is to converse with his inferiors without insolence, and with his superiors with respect and with ease.
~ Doug Stanhope

John was straightforward and respectful with everyone, even with superiors; he wasn't one to swoon over rank. He didn't feel the need to show off or actively seek praise. John was confident enough in himself and his skills that he did his job and let the results speak for themselves. He respected the hierarchy of rank but also understood that, underneath all of the brass, men are men. He could separate the man from the rank and relate to the person as he would anyone, always with respect but on a more equal level. A few CCTs have said that once you are on a team, though rank absolutely matters, ultimately, they're teammates who generally treat each other pretty much as equals.

In 1995, Capt Kurt Buller met SSgt John Chapman. They were both new to the 24, and they got to know each other during training missions with Kurt as team leader and John as ranking NCO. One of Kurt's favorite stories about John was during the same High Risk Survival school incident that Pat Elko shared.

We're probably twenty or twenty-four hours into this training, and we're tired, sitting on one-legged stools, and by this point, because I was the senior ranking officer, they had taken away my fatigues and put me in this kind of like a military laundry sack. They cut the bottom off so it's kind of like a green dress. And I'm walking around in a dress, and everybody else is walking around in fatigues, and they're just trying to belittle me.

So, we're sitting in isolation, and then we hear them start opening up, and you get a sense, 'Ok, it's feeding time," and wait for your turn. They were feeding us three at a time, so they open up, I come crawling out, and I'm sitting there in my skirt, and Johnny Chapman's eating with me along with Johnny Schumacher. And John looks at me, and he just starts chuckling, you know just how he chuckles. They put this bowl of slop down and said, "Eat! Eat now!" So, we sit down, and I'm sitting Indian style, and the whole time, John keeps trying to look under my dress. I said, "Come on, man," trying to cover up, and we're trying to eat, and he kept trying to do this, leaning over to peek, and they're pushing him around like, "Stop it." So finally, I give him a whole look, and he's pulling back and covering his eyes like enough is enough.

So, we get ten to fifteen minutes, and then the three of us go back.

Shortly afterward, the escape attempt happened, and Kurt had to tell the escapees to stand down. "They were crushed because they thought they were doing a good thing. I brought us in together, and we just kinda locked arms and waited for the cadre to come crush us. They came running in and were yelling at us, threatening to kick us out of the course."

Kurt laughed at the memory, "But Johnny trying to look under my dress, I thought that was funny. And then being the team sergeant, telling the other dudes, 'We gotta stick together as a team. Let's bring it in.' It's one of my favorite stories with John, just the sense of humor throughout all of it and then I gave him a full-ball shot, and he got more than he was bargaining for. Every trip we went on, it was the character that John was, the humor, everything was there; he was always just in a good mood even when we were getting crushed."

Col Ken Rodriguez encountered John's humor on occasion, too, but he also saw another side of him. Ken was commander of the 24 when John was killed, and he had a unique vantage point from which to assess the type of man John was. Because he was CCT, they sometimes trained together, so Ken saw the teammate side. As commander, he also was able to see how John was as a subordinate.

One of the things I admired about John is the true humility he had. There's false humility where someone goes, "Aw, it was nothing." John had true humility, and it's not a sign of weakness; it's not a lack of confidence or lack of self-esteem. True humility is a focus outside yourself, whether you focus on the mission, your teammates, your family, your country, or whatever you want to call it, but it's a total lack of focus on yourself—not that John didn't make sure he was an outstanding Combat Controller, he certainly did that, but his focus was never to talk himself up. I could see the characteristics that made John a hero, and I use this term very sparingly. When I use hero, I'm using it in a very strict, very focused way. A true hero is someone who has those characteristics and *then* is presented with those circumstances. John had all those characteristics so it's not like, all of a sudden, "Well, he was made a hero that night." No. He had the character, the values, heroic values, and then when the situation came when presented with the circumstances, all those came to bear; all of them were displayed. He didn't all of a sudden get things he never had before. And where did those values come from? They came from his family and all the way up to his teammates.

Ken contemplated further about John, "I remember, too, another facet of his character and personality was his desire to be extremely competent at his job, which is something we greatly value in this community. In John's case, and hopefully, for most of us, that desire was not for the sake of ego aggrandizement, but so that you will be a very sharp knife or a very capable tool when it's your time to go and do the mission."

When I asked for his thoughts about John from a commander's perspective, Ken started with a little background.

> I remember John was in our Survey Shop. In the Special Tactics world, Survey is going out to potential hot spots all over the world and looking at places where we think, one day, we're going to have to come in and do a mission, or one day we're going to have to rescue people. There are millions of spots all over the world you can say that about. When they look at an area, they have to do it very low-key and look at, "If I have to bring helicopters in here, if I have to land airplanes, if I have to do anything involving air operations, how am I going to do that?" Then you have to translate it all, and John had a high level of expertise in what we call "air integration" as a Combat Controller; he understood things. But you have to translate that to the people who are going to use it who are *not* Combat Controllers and do *not* have all this knowledge. He was skilled in putting things into AutoCAD to draft out these very exacting diagrams of the target area. It takes a fair amount of expertise. Here you have this warrior who's used to "shoot, move, and communicate," and now you have to teach him this very exacting computer

231

program. It takes a lot of expertise to do it right, and it's used by engineers and drafters. It's not "learn this in ten minutes and you can download it off the Internet." It's a pretty involved program. So, John would go out with other surveyors, look at key sites, then distill all of the information down and build this big survey package so anyone in the future could pull it out, look through it, and figure out how they're gonna do what they had to do.

As a commander, one of the things you can do is "leadership by wandering," and I used to wander around the squadron in between all the activities we had. One time, John was working on a survey product; he had just come back from a survey trip. He was the only one in the Survey Shop at the time, so I went in there and said, "Hey, what's up, John?" and he said, "I'm just working on the XXX survey." And then he took the time—he's very, very busy—in the Survey Shop, those guys were *always* tremendously busy. He did more than survey in his career, but at the time of this story, that's where he was. John took the time to walk me through it because *I* don't know how to use AutoCAD; I've never been a Survey guy. So, he walked me through how he turned observations while walking around a field somewhere into this finished product, and he went through the whole thing. Surveys were a big part of our missions, so it was an enormous help for me in understanding that facet, and John just did that. He was good at educating. I remember there was something about

John; he wasn't put off by rank, and he didn't care if you were the commander, or if you were a one-striper, he would get into this "Now I'm in teacher mode, and I'm gonna teach this guy about surveys" and, in this case, it was me. He also thought, "But I do know he's the commander, so there are certain things I will put in there that will help him do his job better." I could see that working in him. Even though I knew John for many years, the one hour I spent in Survey with him that one time was really impactful because it gave me a window into what John's personality was—that teacher part of him, that "I'm going to help *you* be a better commander and understand something."

Ken's story reminds me of when John and Michael not only shared their diving coach with rival schools but also helped teach those divers. John didn't lord his knowledge over others, and he was confident enough in himself that he could share without making the students feel small. What stands out for me is that John didn't just teach Ken the basics of surveying, he also seamlessly included specific information to help him in his role as commander. I'm pretty damn impressed with little brother and I truly wish I had known more about this part of him before he died.

Lt Col Travis Woodworth was a short-term superior of John's. His story reminds me of when John lashed a flashlight to the bumper of his dilapidated tow truck. Travis met John only a few months before he deployed to Afghanistan, but John still left a big impression on him.

At the time, I was a Second Lieutenant at the 24 and the Assistant Team Leader. John was coming over to the team, and my boss was deployed. I was back from my first deployment to Afghanistan and had to fill out the deployment team list. John had been on the team before and left to go to the Survey Team. So, then he was coming back to the team so most of the guys knew him and vouched for him, but one of the things as a team leader is, "I gotta know the men I'm sending down range." John was coming up, and I'm putting him on the playlist, he's on the team to deploy, and I don't know the guy yet.

So, I get him for about, no kidding, two maybe three months before I'm deploying him. He shows up and I start to get to know John; I'm going, "Ok, so where does he fit on the deployment team?" It's kind of a gut check. So, we're going through it, and I look at him and John didn't speak much, and so he's a hard read. I looked at him and John doesn't, so I'm being honest, he doesn't look like the most intellectual guy. So, I start talking to him and he was kinda like a hillbilly savant because once I started talking to him, I realized he was into vehicles, but the details at which he knew vehicles were incredible. Because I'm kind of the same way, when I tie myself into something, I want to know to the Nth degree. You have to understand, technically, I'm his boss and he's gotta know that I kinda know the rules but he took a risk with me because he goes, "Yeah, you know, I was working on my vehicle, and it had this shimmy thing. I kept driving and couldn't figure it out, so I strapped a camera to the axle to see which tire was bouncing."

Back in 2001, we didn't have a lot of equipment, and most people didn't own a camera, so I asked, "What camera?" We spent thousands of dollars on these survey kits and, knowing he came from Survey and they have GPSs, and $5,000 kits. He goes, "Well, I had my survey kit with me so I zip-tied it to the bumper." So, there was a piece of plastic holding on, back then, a $2,500 camera to check whether his wheel was out of balance. I looked at him and I thought, "Oh, boy. So, he used to be smart. I don't know about that anymore." But the fact that he had the gumption, the intuition, the intellect, to go, "Hey, man, here's an option."

I think John "got away" with talking to some superiors like that because of his delivery. It was never an abject disregard for authority. He just spoke to them man-to-man, comfortable with himself and the relationship he had with them, even if it was only for a short time. I have yet to come across someone who says anything to the contrary. John was a man's man who shot from the hip and maybe that served him well most of the time.

As Travis continued to assess John for his deployment list, he thought about the type of man he wanted.

> My analogy was I want the guy who I enter into a basket weaving contest, he's never done basket weaving but I tell him, "You need to win," and I've sold him on the fact that he needs to win. Those guys would get on the Internet and learn how to do it, so when they go do the basket weaving contest, they would win even though they had never done it. So, a tier commander goes, "I want the guy who wants the ball with thirty seconds on the clock and makes the winning shot." When I describe John, I'm going, "He's that guy, but he doesn't want the credit for doing the shot. John definitely *wants* the shot, but he doesn't want the publicity that comes with taking the winning shot. That's what I think about John.

Travis assessed and understood John in a very short and hectic timeframe. He saw in him the same thing we saw as kids. He was the boy who had more assists than goals in soccer because he didn't care who got the recognition; he just wanted the win. Travis was a very astute leader. I don't know if he assigned John to specific teams, but he was definitely lining up the CCT who would be deployed next. The SEAL team to which John was assigned should be thanking God every day that he *was* assigned to them. He saved their lives. Another CCT *might* have done the same thing but changing one factor can change the outcome. A different CCT might have refused to go on such an ill-planned mission. Or maybe another wouldn't have been right behind the leader as they exited the helicopter, enabling him to charge the first bunker. We'll never know, but I am confident that changing *one element* in a situation, any element, would alter the outcome. John's teammates may very well have all been slaughtered had he not been assigned to them.

Whether I spoke with fellow Special Tactics guys, support guys, or leadership, the assessment of John is the same: He was confident, smart, fearless, prepared, and easy to know. Oh, and he still had an enormous head, a cackle laugh, and a stinky ass. Basically, he hadn't changed since childhood.

PART FOUR

Otherworldly Happenings, Posthumous Honors, and a
Sister's Thoughts

They are dead; but they live in each Patriot's breast,
and their names are engraven on honor's bright crest.
~ Henry Wadsworth Longfellow

19

Coincidence or Hand of God?

Coincidence is God's way of remaining anonymous.
~ Albert Einstein

When John first arrived on the island of Okinawa, Japan, he was alone; there were hoops to be jumped through for Valerie to get there. While waiting for her to arrive, John met fellow Controller James Taylor who was also preparing for his family to join him. James and John met on the day they both arrived and decided to bunk together in a two-man room in temporary barracks. James shared the following in an email to me.

> With no TV or anything to keep us [occupied] in that crappy room, we walked around and explored the base. We wound up establishing a tradition of eating soba at the Stars and Stripes lounge and enjoyed talking and telling stories about our lives. Chappy could tell a really good story. While in-processing, I didn't have a lot of time off, so John was in the dorm more than I was. Being that one Bible-believing Christian that everyone

seemed to get "stuck with" sooner or later, I left Christian books lying around; one was a Christian autobiography by Navy SEAL Mickey Block titled *Before the Dawn*. John and I got into conversations about it, and I was impressed by his insight and bold approach to the deepest issues of the spirit this author testified about. I remembered Chappy as a guy who was "really gonna make it." After our wives arrived, we only saw each other occasionally.

I retired in 1995. Fast forward to March 2002: As I sat visiting my in-laws, John's name flashed across the TV screen, and I drove home thinking, "Why him, why a guy like that, Lord?" Later my wife said, "Sometimes the Lord cuts his very elect's time short for His sake." I realized God sometimes brings people to his side because of some special reason, and I think He specifically wants our very own Chappy there to tell his stories, in person, as only he could tell them.

You may be right, James, but whatever the reason, countless people are better off today for having met him—for a short time or a lifetime—and I do believe he is regaling God with some pretty awesome stories. John's faith ran deep. It began when we were young and continued till the day that he laid down his life for others.

Whatever you believe, things happen that cannot be explained except to chalk it up as coincidence or Heavenly intervention. And while I do believe in coincidental occurrences, I also believe God is good, and he sometimes gives us little blessings that we don't recognize until long after they happen. I wish to share some events that happened before and after John was killed. Some allowed people, who normally wouldn't have been able to see him before he deployed, to spend a little time with him. Some are instances of "premonition" before his death or "visits" after. I invite my readers to have an open mind, but I don't expect you'll all see things the way I do. That's fine. I take comfort in my beliefs. My hope is that, at the very least, you are entertained.

Thinking back on John's life, I truly believe he had a guardian angel if not several. He probably needed many because he certainly did enough to keep them busy. I used to say John had nine lives and that was because of things I *knew* about. I've no doubt there are stories we've never heard that might put him at eighteen lives or more. I also imagine many of John's brushes with death were the result of him testing his mettle, pushing the limits, and experiencing *life*. Don't get me wrong: I'm just as certain that many of his dangerous escapades could be chalked up to plain old stupidity, but somehow, he was always none the worse for wear.

Tammy shared something that could have ended John's CCT career before it even started. "It happened sometime in 1988 or early 1989 at his Peoria Street apartment in Aurora. David and I went to visit him not long after he had been working on his 1971 Pontiac Bonneville, and he told us what had happened to him. John had the engine lifted out of the front end so he could work on something beneath it. As he leaned under the heavy motor, he heard a voice at his shoulder that sounded like our grandfather John Kennedy (not *that* John Kennedy). The voice said, "Better get your hands out of there." When John pulled away and turned toward the voice, the engine fell where his hands had just been.

John was destined for bigger things. If the engine had fallen on him, I don't know if he could have been killed, but the likelihood of him fulfilling his dream of becoming a Combat Controller is probably pretty low. At the very least, it would have taken him a long time to recover and not to the level he'd need to be as CCT. I believe God spoke to him that day through the trusted voice of our deceased grandfather.

In November 1990, John and Valerie went to Dad and Tess's house in Michigan to go hunting up north with Dad. Before heading to the camp, they went for a horseback ride. Tess remembers, "We were all just walking the horses slowly and talking about nothing much. All of a sudden, John's horse bucked him off without any warning." A horsefly had bitten his horse and, in an effort to rid itself of the offender, it sent John ass-end-over-teakettle. He got up, dusted himself off, and they continued their ride.

After turning the horses out to pasture, the three packed up and headed to the camp. They arrived too late for anything but dinner and hitting the rack, with the plan of getting up early to start the hunt. In the wee hours of the morning, John woke Valerie, telling her he was in incredible pain. Valerie remembers, "I checked him and his stomach was enlarged. I immediately knew we needed to get him to the hospital. I've never seen John with tears in his eyes; he was in so much pain." They loaded John into the truck and headed out to the hospital, but Dad, not familiar with the area, went in the wrong direction. By the time he figured it out, they'd gone fifteen minutes the wrong way. He turned around and hightailed it to the hospital. When the ER doctor examined John, he shook his head and said, "You're one lucky dude. If you had waited *any* longer, you'd be dead." John had ruptured his spleen.

He spent a few days in the hospital, and since he wasn't cleared to fly, Dad drove him home to North Carolina. Though he didn't need surgery to remove the spleen, John *was* sidelined from physical activities for six months. He was given all manner of non-physical assignments, one of which also almost cost him his life. He missed Desert Storm because of his injury. Was he saved for bigger things, or was his life just saved? Perhaps it's both and this time he was assigned an angel on Earth—Valerie, his personal nurse.

While on light duty due to his spleen injury, John was part of a two-man team on the ground during drop zone and assault zone training at Fort Bragg. They were to be ground crew near the drop zone where enormous payloads should, theoretically, land. The contents of the drop were huge—perhaps a truck or tank or some other mammoth vehicle. As he and his teammate sat in their vehicle waiting for the drop, they weren't paying attention to the descending beast. They had parked far enough away from the landing zone to qualify as a safe distance but sometimes "far enough" isn't really. John told me that the payload slammed mere yards from their truck, and the shockwave rocked it so much they thought it would flip over. Had it landed on their vehicle, neither would have survived. Is that dumb luck or something else entirely?

When the terrorist attacks happened on September 11, 2001, I was working two jobs: a full-time position at the courthouse and part-time for UPS at Bradley Airport. John was sent to Virginia Beach pretty quickly to start training with a SEAL team, so he was there on Veteran's Day weekend in November. Since the courthouse was a state job, we had the Monday of that weekend off. My schedule at UPS was Tuesday to Saturday, so I already had Monday off. With no school on Veteran's Day either, I told Mom that Rachel and I were using the weekend to go see John. I didn't know if I'd have another opportunity to see him before he deployed, and it was the best weekend for my schedule. She immediately said she'd join us.

We left right after my UPS shift ended on Saturday morning and drove to Grandma Kennedy's house in New Jersey for a quick stopover. Knowing we wouldn't have a lot of time with John, we pressed on, arriving at his apartment after dark. While Rachel slept, Mom and I stayed up with him, talking about anything and everything. Because of the early hours I worked and the long trip to Virginia Beach, I was exhausted and, try as I might to stay awake, the soft cushions of the couch finally sucked me in and coaxed me into a deep slumber. Mom and John stayed up a while longer still talking about anything that came to mind.

The next day, John took us to the Virginia Aquarium to get out of the apartment. It was a relaxing day with him, and Rachel thoroughly enjoyed the exhibits. Our time together was much too short, and we knew it. I told John, "Be careful and watch your back." I left some thoughts unspoken. I didn't want to say anything that might put doubt in his head. I feared that if I planted even the tiniest seed of doubt, it would create danger in the situations I imagined he'd face. What I *wanted* to do was grab onto him and beg him not to go. Instead, I told him, "I love you, and I am so very proud of you." I needed him to know, out loud, how I felt.

During our all-too-brief visit, we found out that John didn't *have* to deploy with the SEAL team; he *chose* to go because he felt it was the right thing to do. He didn't necessarily want to go to war, but he chose to deploy with them because, as he said, "They trained with me; they know how to work with me. Sending them with someone else could increase personal danger for them or invite possible mistakes because of unfamiliarity." *That's* the kind of man and teammate John was—honorable, even when it meant going where he didn't want to go. But he *did* want to go.

Monday, Veteran's Day, was a very difficult and emotional day. We had to leave after breakfast to make it back in time for me to get a little rest before heading to UPS at 3:00 a.m. Tuesday morning. We dragged out our goodbyes as long as we could. Saying goodbye was *not* easy, especially when I had a gut-wrenching, awful feeling about leaving John. He was stoic and quick with giant bear hugs. Did I tell you he gave great hugs? I don't think I'd be too far off to imagine he was a bit sad to watch us drive away. I am so thankful to have had that blur of a weekend with John, Rachel, and Mom, but the awful, unspoken feeling in the pit of my stomach foreshadowed events to come.

The terrible feeling continued into December. We used to do an adult gift draw every Christmas, and I drew John's name. I will *never* forget exactly how I felt as I wrapped his present. I had been so excited when I found it—a Harley Davidson hitch cover for his shiny new Silverado pickup. The truck was black, with an extended cab and a five-foot bed; it was John's pride and joy. I knew he'd love his new truck accessory, but as I wrapped the hitch cover, I cried—no, I *bawled*—as a thought kept repeating in my head, "He's not even going to get to use this." What should have been a happy little activity turned into an upsetting task because somewhere deep within, I knew something bad was ahead. I could feel it.

I never expected to see John again before his deployment because he and Valerie had planned on going to her parents' house in Pennsylvania for Christmas. At the last minute, they decided to stop at Grandma Kennedy's house in Trenton so anyone who could make it there could see them. Mom, Rachel, and I made the three-and-a-half-hour trip from Windsor Locks. Our visit was only two days, but I am thankful to have had them. I got to watch John play with Madison and Brianna, comb their silky blonde hair after he gave them a bath, and cuddle with them in the chair while he read books to them. His little family posed for photos just before they headed to Pennsylvania. It was the last time Mom, Grandma, Rachel, or I saw John. If they hadn't made a last-minute change to their plans, we wouldn't have seen them at all that Christmas. I am thankful for their eleventh-hour detour.

As the time drew near for John to deploy, Tammy called him with news that she would be flying into Raleigh Airport on a very rare business trip; this might have been her one and only. John drove the hour and twenty minutes to see her at the hotel. They visited in her room, talking about anything and everything, most of which remain Tammy's private memories, but she did share one cute tidbit. John reached into his pocket and pulled out one or two of his girls' hair ties; they called them *ponies*. They were his little treasures, and he often had some wherever he went. He deployed with a couple of ponies in his pocket, reminders of his two little girls.

John took Tammy out for lunch where they continued their brother/sister conversation. Tammy remembers when John brought her back to the hotel, "We said goodbye in front of the hotel. We hugged tightly then he got into his truck. The last time I saw his face was when he was driving away. He looked in his driver's side mirror, it was large, so I could see his full face, and I didn't see his usual happy smile. Instead, his expression was somber, and as I waved to him, I had a heavy heart." There's no way either of them could know what was to come, but it seems apparent that both had a sense of foreboding.

If Tammy hadn't been sent on that unusual business trip, and if John hadn't decided he had time to meet her, she would not have seen him before he deployed.

John's SEAL team was scheduled to deploy in early January 2002, but he couldn't go with them because our Grandma Chapman had died unexpectedly. She was almost ninety years old but still in good health. He asked to deploy with his team, but the commander insisted he wait until after Grandma's funeral. One of his CCT brothers had volunteered to go in his place. John was torn; he wanted to go with his team, but he knew going to Michigan was the right thing to do.

Grandma's death brought mourners from near and far, including Kevin, so John was able to spend time with relatives he normally wouldn't have seen, and there were a lot. I couldn't go because of my two jobs. Tammy was not able to attend either because she had little ones at home. Dad and Tess lived in Belding, a small town less than two hours from the cemetery in Flint, so Kevin and John stayed with them and relatives gathered there to remember Grandma.

When John returned from Michigan, it became his mission to get put back with his team. Since he had been replaced, he'd have to sit on the sidelines until another team needed a CCT. As fate would have it, John's replacement received some sad news of his own; his mother-in-law had passed, and the commander sent him to be with *his* wife and family. And just like that, John was back on the team.

Had Grandma Chapman not died when she did, Dad, Tess, Kevin, and so many of our Michigan relatives would never have seen John before he left for Afghanistan. And if his replacement hadn't then also had a family death, John would not have gone with that team and may possibly have returned home alive. But he also wouldn't have been there to single-handedly save twenty-three men on the deadly morning of March 4, 2002.

Madison was almost six when John deployed for the last time. He was expected back around April 15, 2002. She had developed a little ritual, a special gift for John, on some of his previous deployments. She loved building with LEGOs®, and when Valerie told her, "Daddy's coming home," Madison would build a castle for him to see when he walked in the door. On March 3, 2002, she set about building a castle for John's return. When Valerie asked what she was doing, she replied, "Building Daddy's castle." Val told her, "Daddy's not coming home yet; not for another month." Without looking up from her LEGO® castle, Madison said in her tiny voice, "No, he's coming home."

Valerie told us that on one of the first few nights after John's death, she laid down on the bed they had shared, exhausted from a myriad of emotions and so many taxing decisions. As she curled onto her side facing the edge of the bed and sleep crept in, she felt someone lay down behind her, spooning her, hugging her. When Valerie rolled over to see who it might be, the bed was empty. She strained to see in the dark and could barely make out John's torso lying next to her. In an instant, it was gone. Was it an exhaustion-induced hallucination or was John saying, "I am with you?"

In an effort to escape her somber home, and perhaps to feel "normal," if only for a couple of hours, Valerie went out to a club with close friends several days after John was killed. As she and a couple of friends took the dance floor, another watched from their table. He looked twice because he couldn't believe what he saw. On the dance floor next to Valerie, he saw the shadow of someone dancing with her, yet no one was there. It was brief but long enough for him to know he wasn't just seeing things.

In March 2002, Mike West was still rotating in and out of Afghanistan. I asked him something you're probably not supposed to ask a warrior. If not, he forgave my ignorance. I asked him if he and John had ever talked about the possibility of one of them not coming home. His answer didn't really surprise me.

> No. You don't ever think it's going to happen to you. Of course, I never thought it would happen to John.

After his death, I had a couple of close calls when I was in Afghanistan, and I felt like I was protected. I sometimes wonder if he was watching over me. I watched a truck blow up in front of me. I watched guys fly out of the truck. After that, people were shooting at me, and I never felt really scared. I felt very strong and felt like, man, I had a purpose in life. And I also felt like I was very protected. And I look back on it and I'm like, "Man, why did I feel that way?" and I wonder if it was John, or somebody else. One day I'll know, there's no doubt in my mind.

As we were wrapping up our conversation, Mike said,

I talk to him. I talk to him when I'm working on the car [the Cobra], and I think it's more of knowing that he's proud of it, but it's just kind of buddy-talk—that he wouldn't want it any other way. He'd want me to talk like he was standing there beside me, having a beer with me. That's it; nothing special about it. It's funny, I've talked to him many times while working on the car.

One day my wife Paola talked me into going with her and her mother to see a psychic. It was in a shady part of town and she didn't want to go alone. Reluctantly, I said yes, but I also thought it would be entertaining, especially when they start asking, "Do you have a family member whose name begins with the letter "M" or something like that.

There was a room full of people and we were sitting three rows back. I was on the outskirts at the far end of the row. As this unique-looking, bare-footed black lady walked in and started talking to the group, I couldn't have cared less; I was on my phone doing other things. She began talking about how the gallery reading was going to go and I looked up a few times. She kept looking at me. Quietly, I closed my phone and put it away. I didn't want to get called out. As I sat there, she kept looking my way. I was thinking, "What's going on???" She explained that she would do the readings starting from the front of the room and then move to the next person. All of a sudden, she stopped giving instructions and looked directly at me again. She announced that she had to talk to the guy in the back because this guy was coming through and would not stop bugging her. At that moment, she walked over to me and stopped. She promptly saluted me and started telling me that I had received a vehicle from a friend. I didn't acknowledge or disclaim her statement, but she continued. This lady then told me I have a mancave where I work on this vehicle and that "my friend" can hear me when I talk to him. She even told me his Air Force nametag sits in the car. She then went on to tell me that there is a replica of this car above my TV. I had never spoken about any of this to anyone prior to that meeting and it took some time afterward to tell others … after my wife would put me on the spot to tell our friends what happened at the gallery reading.

There's no doubt in my mind he's in my heart and he's with me. I feel a huge attachment to him like he's sitting right there with me. John's life is a part of me, and I don't let it bring me down; I let it inspire me.

Dave Gendron had a war story similar to Mike's. He was in Afghanistan not long after John died, and he was driving a Humvee when they were attacked. Bullets were flying, one of them hitting the back of his seat. It should have penetrated the cushion and entered Dave's body but for reasons unknown, it did not. He said he "felt" someone there, protecting him that day.

There they are—several stories that may or may not be indicators of something "more" in this world. They might be mere coincidence or orchestrations from God, but no matter what they truly are or what any of us think, they happened. And I am thankful that they did.

20

Posthumous Honors

No one is actually dead until the ripples they cause in the world die away.
-~ Terry Pratchett, author of *Reaper Man*

No one could have predicted the outpouring of honors in John's name after he was killed. He would be humbled by it all. Every thoughtful gesture bestowed upon him warms my heart. More than two decades after his death, and the many years in between, countless people and groups have come up with unique ways to pay homage to John. Every honor is special—from the biggest to the smallest—and if I can shine a light on them, I will. John was not a braggart. By now, it has been well established that he didn't need accolades to shore up his self-worth. But he's not here anymore, and I have no qualms over crowing about my brother. I think the sheer number of honors is testimony to who he was and what he meant to so many. Please indulge me as I share the numerous and cool ways people chose to recognize and honor John.

Immediately after his death, and before his funeral in Pennsylvania, the 24 honored John with a beautiful memorial service in their compound's cavernous parachute packing facility. It was standing room only. Honestly, I don't remember a whole lot about the ceremony; the newness of accepting I'd never hug John again or hear his famous cackle-laugh even one more time numbed my brain, but I do remember the enormous flag that was used as the backdrop. It amazed me that one could be so big. It's strange the things you *do* remember. I didn't know until Kenny told me recently that the 24 opened their gates to all who were serving on Pope AFB and lots of people came to pay their respects for a man they never knew. He also said, "The guy who beautifully sang the National Anthem was assigned to Pope and didn't bat an eye when I asked him if he would sing it. He said, 'I would be honored.' He was awesome." The only thing I recollect about the anthem is his angelic voice and that it made me cry. Thank you, then-TSgt Marvin Gregory for honoring John without hesitation.

After everyone found a spot, I looked around to see tears falling from manly men who hugged as brothers do. I appreciated those tears. I don't know who spoke; I don't know what was said, but my takeaway was that the people of the 24 and Pope AFB loved John as a brother. I appreciated that too. To all who were there, from the bottom of my heart, thank you.

One of the most cherished honors to John is a poem written by our mom. She has never set pen to paper, but the poem came to her in bits and pieces throughout one restless night. She tried to ignore it, but the words kept coming, so she got up each time and wrote them down. In the morning, after a little rearranging, she had her masterpiece.

Treasure the Memories

There are so many stories
About this little boy
Although you were a rascal
You brought your family joy.
From bikes in trees and lightning bolts
And giggles in the dark,
Little League and soccer games
And picnics in the park.

God blessed you with the gift
Of a tender, loving heart.
There are so many stories,
I wouldn't know where to start.
You touched so many lives
With your caring gentle ways.
You helped so many people
And brightened many days.

Green Giant, Mame and diving boards;
Some high school things to do
Tried college, cars and tow trucks,
Then Air Force time for you.
You branched to Special Forces
And wore a red beret.
Proud parents, friends and you

Did celebrate that day.
The love of your life was met
On a trip that you took with Joe.
You made her a wife, then mother,
And your family began to grow.
A dog, little girls, and Barbie dolls
And splashing in the pool.
You loved your cutie patooties.
Your heart they soon did rule.

You went to war for freedom
And there you gave your life.
You leave behind your treasures,
Your daughters and your wife.
These precious three live on
As special parts of you.
We'll love them and protect them
As we know you would do.

Scrapbooks and snapshots
Homemade movies too,
Help to keep the memories
That we have of you.
Scrapbooks and snapshots,
They will have to do
Until the day will come again
When we can be with you.

Terry Chapman, 2002

Mom was surprised by how quickly these words came, and she felt they were a gift from God—a way for her to remember the little things about John's life.

In May 2002, only two months after John saved his team, the Navy SEALs acknowledged his actions and declared him one of their heroes by adding his name to the wall of honor at their Dam Neck compound in Virginia Beach. It is three panels of shiny, black stone set in front of a curved line of green shrubbery. The middle portion is taller than the two angled flanking wings, and John's name is on the left panel at the bottom of a list of fallen SEALs. His is the only non-SEAL, non-Navy name etched into the stone. On the surface, it was an enormous honor, and maybe it truly was meant that way, but the ceremony solidified the belief, at least for me, that there was more to the story than we had been told. As more information has come out over the years, I now look back on the gesture with great cynicism regarding their motives, especially after all they've done since then. I still struggle to find forgiveness that may never come so, perhaps, for now, instead of viewing it as a way to appease their collective conscience or to camouflage wrongdoing, it's best to just accept it as a great honor because it is, no matter the motivation behind it. Including John's name on a Navy SEAL wall speaks volumes without uttering a word.

While the Air Force was dissecting what had gone wrong, my brother-in-law David found an outlet for his grief by working on his own tribute. To honor the friend and brother who introduced him to Tammy, David turned the pain he felt over losing John into a beautiful ballad called *Love That Holds My Heart*. The raw emotion of his grief and the pride he has for John are evident in the words. David recorded himself singing lead, harmony, and playing each instrument, and then mixed the recordings into an amazing, heartfelt song. I wish I could insert it on this page for you to hear. I bawl every time. Though I can't listen to it often because of how deeply it affects me, there are times I *want* to hear it and cry because it's a cathartic release of the pain that never goes away. I imagine that writing the lyrics and the process of creating the song gave David a similar kind of release. It is one of my favorite tributes to John.

I hope by now, having read this far into John's life, you have some understanding of how much he affected others. If you need more convincing, lean into this story about the memorial erected in our hometown. I covered it a bit in *Alone at Dawn*, but this is the complete story.

The 7-and-a-half-hour trip from Hartford, Connecticut, to Windber, Pennsylvania, started in silence. It was March 11, 2002, and Brian Topor, David Wrabel, and Mike Toce were on their way to say goodbye forever to their best childhood friend. They hadn't seen John much after he joined the Air Force, but he always took time to see them when he was in town. Those visits seemed a lifetime ago, and they were trying to process never seeing him again. They laughed a lot during the trip, remembering the fun times they'd all had with him. Before long, talk turned to honoring John and never letting his memory fade. They came to a collective conclusion, "This *can't* be it; this *can't* be forever for Chappy." They were not about to let his legacy grow silent.

The four boys had been in the same classes most years of school. They attended St. Robert's Church CCD (Confraternity of Christian Doctrine, which is religious education for youngsters) and made their First Holy Communions and Confirmations together. They played on the same soccer teams and ran with the same group of neighborhood kids. The boys became the men they are now, together, challenging each other in ways only close friendships can. When Brian, David, and Michael came together in mourning and in celebration of their beloved friend, the idea of a memorial in his honor was a natural next step. A funeral service *couldn't* be the end for Chappy.

Their brainstorming ran the gamut—renaming Bradley International Airport, renaming a stretch of highway, or a building—and ended with the decision to erect a memorial near the high school soccer field where they had all played. By the time they made it back to Connecticut, their plan was formulated, though they couldn't have imagined what it would take to make their vision a reality. Brian remembers,

> We thought that keeping the memorial in town was the most meaningful, but we also thought that since Chappy wasn't buried in Windsor Locks, we wanted a place for people to go and remember him. And we did it for his mom too. After deciding on a memorial

at the high school, we knew from that moment that it *had* to be by the soccer field. We didn't know anything else—legalities, rules, permissions—we just said, "This is what we're going to do," and we approached it with the attitude that there was no other possible outcome; it *would* happen.

They accomplished in only seven months (March to October 2002) what seasoned organizers couldn't do in twice that time. Other friends wanted to help, so they created a committee to spread the workload. Included on the committee were lifelong friends and neighbors, Skeeter Tersavich and Celeste (Letendre) Lefebvre, who felt the same draw to honor John as the others did. Celeste's husband Steven played an integral part as foreman in the planning and physical creation of the memorial. John's classmates and friends Joanne Kryszpin and Kenny Loughran were valued voices at committee meetings and unstoppable forces in mobilizing their efforts. Rounding out the core committee was Coach Sullivan and Tom Allen. Mom and I attended the meetings to offer input but left the vision to the friends who loved John enough to put their lives on hold to follow their hearts. We are in awe of these people.

To fund the memorial and its long-term preservation, the committee held a fundraiser in August 2002 at the Knights of Columbus. HARP Mechanical, Windsor Locks Lions Club, and the Windsor Locks Safety Complex used their billboards to advertise the event: "John Chapman Memorial Benefit: August 18, 2-8 p.m."

Brian praises Kenny Loughran, "He was one of the unsung heroes of the whole thing. He got out of work and then hit the streets, going door-to-door, block-by-block, seeking donations. He was amazing. He raised an enormous amount of money on his own volition." The Savage Brothers, a rock band primarily made up of Windsor Locks men, one of whom was in John's graduating class, volunteered their talent to the fundraiser. Businesses from Windsor Locks and surrounding towns donated gifts to be raffled, from two Southwest Airlines round-trip tickets to Red Sox tickets and certificates from local restaurants. So many raffle items were received (over 100) that it took an hour to get through them all. An 86° day with 76% humidity didn't keep friends and strangers from showing up to support the effort. Three Air Force members even drove from Massachusetts to attend. One of them, TSgt Jay Lemley, told me in a "small world" story that he had worked with John at Pope AFB. The community came together to honor one of their own. A slideshow of photos ended with a short video John had sent Mom several years earlier. He was sitting on his couch, and the last thing he said, looking directly into the camera, was, "I'll see you in August." Tears flowed in the silent room on that hot August day.

While the committee organized the fundraiser, they simultaneously constructed the memorial. A local company donated the rock, and Coach Sullivan found one with a surface flat enough for a plaque. It must have looked like a comedy show: Sullivan chose one rock and it was put onto a truck. "No, not that one. How about the one over there?" So off came the first and on went the second. There were several "ons-and-offs" before he found the perfect rock. The committee added a flagpole that extends up from behind the stone—thirty feet tall and topped by a golden eagle.

Countless people came out to help with the manual labor, including John's "other dad" Stanley Topor. John had spent so much time with Brian at the Topor household that he was like a son to Stanley. The flagpole and rock are encircled by pavers, which, back then, were framed with shrubs, two trees, and pretty flowers, leaving an opening for visitors. The trees are no longer there, but flowers (when the season is right) and shrubs remain.

After first calling "North Carolina" and asking for a number to the base there, and after a speaking with a dozen other people, David finally got in touch with First Sergeant Kenny Longfritz. They needed the squadron's emblem for inclusion on the plaque. That was easy. Then Kenny surprised David when he asked if they wanted some of the team to parachute into the ceremony. "Uh, yeah!" On October 19, 2002, after joking about almost losing their jobs and getting divorced because of their dedication to the project, the committee stood back and marveled at the idea that had become reality. The official unveiling was a ceremony like no other in Windsor Locks. Local and state dignitaries came, family and friends spoke, and a large crowd gathered to celebrate John. His teammates were not able to jump into the event due to overcast and sprinkling skies, so they stood on a hill and watched. Kenny and MSgt Mike Rizzuto, both in their dress blues, slowly raised the flag as the

266

Windsor Locks High School marching band played the National Anthem. Ironically, the sun shone brightly as the ceremony came to a close.

I hosted a party at my house that evening so everyone could blow off steam after seven months of balls-to-the-wall effort, and that is when a mutual interest began between Kenny and me.

Years later, I was talking with Brian, David, and Mike "Coma" Toce (so nicknamed by Kenny) about the memorial and what it meant to them and to the town. At the time, Mike worked for an OBGYN who brought his son to the dedication. Mike said, "The boy was young at the time, but he was so inspired by what he witnessed and by what he learned that he ended up attending Westpoint and becoming an Army Special Ops operator." Well done, Sir, and thank you for your service!

John's name has found its way onto many street signs—possibly some in places I haven't discovered. In conjunction with the memorial at our high school, the town renamed the street leading into Veteran's Park to TSgt John A. Chapman Way. There is also Chapman Boulevard in Kyrgyzstan, John Chapman Parkway on Nellis AFB, Nevada, Chapman Circle on MacDill AFB in Tampa, Florida, and Chapman Loop on the JSOC compound on Fort Bragg in North Carolina. The passenger terminal at Bagram Airfield in Afghanistan was dedicated to John. Before the ill-planned and tragic exit of American forces, guys painted over the dedication so it would not be desecrated after they left.

Stronghold Chapman was a Forward Operating Base (FOB) in Iraq, and Kurt Buller taught youngsters in a classroom he nicknamed FOB Chapman.

John's story has been recounted in magazines like *Newsweek, Time, VFW Magazine,* and *Stuff.* Print and online newspapers, way too many to name, have covered John's story over the years. I do want to single out Charlene McMahon, a freelance writer in Connecticut, who became a dear friend while asking us to share a bit of John during the worst time in our lives. We weren't just an exclusive story for her like so many families of the fallen; she respected our pain and never pushed for anything we weren't willing or able to give. Charlene is a true journalist and a wonderful friend.

John's actions on March 4, 2002, were submitted for the Air Force Cross not long after he was killed. It seemed to be taking an inordinate amount of time for the Air Force to present an award, especially since we learned that Pararescueman SrA Jason Cunningham, who was also killed on Takur Ghar in the follow-on battle to take the mountain, was awarded the Air Force Cross in September. Our family was told that the delay was caused by certain top officials questioning if the award shouldn't be the Medal of Honor. That was another indication to me that there was more to the story than we had been told up to that point.

Ultimately, John was posthumously awarded the Air Force Cross on January 10, 2003, at Pope AFB. Held in a giant hangar, with the mammoth American flag as a backdrop, the ceremony drew top Air Force brass, but that's not what pulled at my heart. Behind us was a sea of men wearing scarlet, maroon, and gray berets, as well as countless civilians and veteran CCT and PJs. Several of John's childhood friends traveled from Connecticut to witness his award. It was standing room only. *That's* what meant the most to me; seeing those who came from near and far to honor him.

During the three or four days we were in North Carolina for the Air Force Cross ceremony, my relationship with Kenny continued to blossom, and we spent every waking moment together. We had been long-distance dating since the Windsor Locks ceremony, and he took giant detours to see me on his way to Buffalo Bills games in New York. He also came up for a very brief visit at Christmas. He just couldn't stay away! Our closeness didn't go unnoticed by some at the 24. Kenny was already on terminal leave (getting ready to retire), allowing him time to show me around. We ran into Combat Controller and funnyman Kyle Stanbro. He got serious and told Kenny, "Hey, I'm not so sure I like the new first sergeant's policy." Tim Laughner was Kenny's temporary replacement. Always looking out for his men but not sure what could have changed in such a short time, Kenny was concerned, "What policy?" Kyle leaned toward us and said, "Before we deploy, now we have to leave him photos of our sisters." He snapped his head in my direction, "Too soon?" After a second of "what did he just say," with Kenny holding his breath and thinking, "I can't believe he just said that," we burst out laughing. Only Kyle! I love that guy!

I left North Carolina on Monday, not wanting to part from Kenny. He brought us to the airport and said he'd see me soon. He came to Connecticut sooner than I expected, showing up that Thursday, using the ruse of wanting to give me an early birthday gift—a DVD player since I didn't have one. He also bought a card and a dozen roses and placed them on the coffee table in front of me. I read the card, "Look into the roses for your future." I think my jaw hit my knees as I asked, "What did you do?" Tucked into the roses was a small, velveteen box. Kenny asked, "Will you marry me?" I don't really want to admit it, but my immediate response was, "Shit yeah." I slapped a hand over my mouth and begged for a do-over. Too late. It was done.

We both felt as though John had somehow brought us together. We were married in June 2003, surrounded by beloved family and friends. The men in the wedding party wore pins with John's photo, and on the back of our wedding program, we thanked God and John for leading us to each other.

In a small ceremony on March 31, 2004, a life-size mannequin in John's likeness was unveiled in the Enlisted Heritage Hall, TSgt John A. Chapman Exhibition, at the Gunter Annex of Maxwell AFB in Montgomery, Alabama. Madison and Brianna looked so tiny as they gazed up at the mannequin that resembled their daddy, and I wondered what they understood about him then. The display depicts John in desert camo, wearing his

CCT headset, and carrying his weapon. At his feet is a scarlet beret folded over combat boots and the now-famous photo of him with the little Afghan girl.

In March 2005, a massive art exhibit opened at the Women in Military Memorial in Arlington National Cemetery. Close to 200 talented artists from all corners of the country contributed portraits to honor the more than 1,300 US military men and women killed in Iraq and Afghanistan up to that point. John's portrait, painted by Martha Spurlock, is among the other men who died that same day. When we visited the exhibit, we found two notes left for John. One read, "John Chapman, you are Windsor Locks' hero. We salute you. The students of Windsor Locks Middle School 6/3/05." The other note was just as special, short, and to the point: "Chappie, we honor you. Tailpipe Charlie, Combat Control School, Pope."

Next is something that would have completely tickled John pink. On April 8, 2005, the MV Merlin was re-commissioned the MV TSgt John A. Chapman at Sunny Point in North Carolina. The irony of it wouldn't have escaped John. It is a privately-owned munitions ship, leased by the Navy, docked at an Army base, and named for an airman who, it just so happens, relied on those munitions to carry out his missions of wreaking havoc on the enemy. The MV Chapman is an impressive vessel. John would be humbled, but let's face it, having a ship named after you is pretty freakin' awesome!

Around 2006, the Combat Control Association (CCA) started sponsoring an award given to a student graduating from the Special Tactics Training Squadron

(STTS). The John A. Chapman Award is a beautiful wooden plaque with a miniature statue of John in his CCT gear offset to the left side of the wood. According to Mike Lamonica, once students graduate Combat Control School, they move on to STTS for combat readiness training. The award is voted on by all students and, as is printed on the plaque, "Presented to the graduating AST [Advanced Skills Training] student who best exemplifies the attributes of a "team player" by continually putting others before himself, keeping the team together, and always striving for mission success." Congratulations to all who have earned this award over the years. John would be proud of you.

It's difficult to say what tribute is the best, but my personal favorite has to be our son. After one miscarriage and Kenny accepting that he just wasn't meant to be a dad, I found myself pregnant once more. Without discussion, we independently decided if it was a boy, he would be named after John. In March 2006, we welcomed John Chapman Longfritz, and he has been a challenge and a joy ever since. Having never raised a boy, I discovered that they can be gross little creatures but also so much fun! After raising Rachel and answering girl questions for her, I figured the boy questions would go to Kenny. No such luck! John had a habit of waiting for the two of us to be in the car and on the road before he started with, "Mom, can I ask you something?" By now, I expect *anything* to fall out of his mouth, but when it first happened, my grip tightened on the steering wheel; I was paralyzed for an instant. My panicked eyes stared straight ahead as my mind raced for the words to answer his random question about sex or babies or puberty. I thought, "WHY didn't he ask Kenny?" My philosophy is that if a child of any age is aware enough to ask a question, he or she is owed an honest answer at the level he/she can comprehend. So, after my moment of paralysis, I answered him bluntly and truthfully. He still catches me off guard at times, but I love that he feels he can ask or tell me anything (so far). John wears his heart on his sleeve. He is kind and funny and very smart and was blessed with the God-given gift of music. There's no accordion in his repertoire, but he did quite well on piano and violin when he was younger, and still picks up his electric and acoustic guitars when he has time.

As Kenny, Rachel, and I were getting used to having a tiny, new human in our family, the Air Force was preparing to host their Basic Military Training 60th Anniversary celebration at Lackland AFB in San Antonio, Texas. The celebration honored their enlisted heroes. On June 14, 2006, they named buildings after several deserving airmen; John was one of them. The Chapman Training Complex housed dorm rooms, training rooms, and a display that chronicled the events of John's battle on Takur Ghar. I've met many people since then who lived in the Chapman Training Complex or who were in awe of seeing it. John would probably be embarrassed, "Man, I was just doing what I had to do."

In 2009, I did what I had to do; I got myself a portrait tattoo of John on the back of my left shoulder. It is a photo of him when he graduated Combat Control School. I wanted the tattoo to be black-and-gray except for the red beret because it needed to stand out like John did.

When I showed our three-year-old, asking him who it was, John immediately responded, "Uncle John." I was relieved! Tattoos are permanent … and can go so wrong.

Windsor Locks townie Anthony Burke also got ink that honors John. It is an eagle head with a battle-torn American flag behind it. It reads, "In memory of J.C." Thank you, Anthony, for honoring John in such a permanent way.

Ken Rodriguez shared something with me that I hadn't heard before. He was a fulltime JROTC instructor at Pensacola High School in 2011 when they started running the Northwest Florida Junior ROTC Summer Leadership School (SLS) at Hurlburt Field. The program, which to this date, has conducted 13 annual programs since its inception, is focused on leadership, teamwork, and accountability. No longer a fulltime JROTC instructor, Ken now heads up the program as a volunteer with a team of JROTC instructors along with military and civilian volunteers. This amazing program is sponsored by the 1st Special Operations Wing, HQ Air Force Junior ROTC, and Escambia County School District—and currently involves cadets from seven area high schools in and around Hurlburt Field. The days are long and full of physical and mental challenges. As Ken explained, it's kind of a cross between Outward Bound and military boot camp squeezed into an intense 5-day/4-night program.

In 2023, the traditional encampment area on Hurlburt Field was moved from open-bay barracks to a mini "tent city" on Hurlburt. With Valerie's blessing, the 24 SOW and 1 SOW named their new encampment area Camp Chapman in honor of John. Along with the many blocks of instruction, the cadets get a detailed lesson on MSgt John Chapman and his heroic deeds and sacrifices during Operation Anaconda, Afghanistan.

Having known Ken for over twenty years, I can say with certainty that this amazing program will give its participants skills they may not have received otherwise. Good luck to all the young people fortunate enough to attend the Northwest Florida Junior ROTC Summer Leadership School. Listen to your mentors! They will not steer you wrong.

On August 22, 2018, after sixteen years and many painful obstacles that should never have happened, John's Air Force Cross was finally upgraded to the Medal of Honor in a ceremony officiated by President Donald Trump. John became the first enlisted airman since Vietnam to earn our nation's highest military honor and is also the first to have video proof of his actions. In the two days following the Medal of Honor ceremony, John was inducted into the Pentagon Hall of Heroes, and his name was prominently displayed on the Air Force Memorial in Washington, DC.

On the Tuesday before the Medal of Honor ceremony, the family and CCT escorts were given a tour of the Pentagon. It's an enormous and impressive building full of very special people. On the way back to

General David Goldfein's office (then-Air Force Chief of Staff), which was approximately 0.7 miles, hundreds of people lined the halls, clapping as we walked by. Some mouthed, "Thank you," and others were crying. After realizing what was going on, I cried and thanked those who caught my gaze. It was the most emotional part of that entire week—the outpouring of love and support was overwhelming. People who didn't even work at the Pentagon wanted to participate.

Wednesday, the day of the medal ceremony, was almost surreal. We were escorted to the East Wing of the White House where we were serenaded by a trio from the Air Force Band. My son cannot stay still when music is playing so he started dancing. When a staffer walked by, he quickly stopped, and she said, "Don't stop. How many people can say they danced in the East Wing of the White House?" Indeed! John was happy to resume his fancy footwork.

When we were led into the East Room, I was surprised at how small it is. Television makes it look so much bigger, but it is a pretty room, elegant. We sat on white cushioned chairs and waited while invited guests arrived. As President Trump posthumously awarded the Medal of Honor, I felt satisfaction more than anything else. The truth of John's actions was publicly acknowledged, and his level of award finally reflected the heroism he showed on that desolate mountaintop. It has always been very important to me that people know, though it would never have been to him. John would shrug, say he was just doing his job, and then recognize the other warriors who paid the ultimate price that day. I think of them often and honor them every March 4, just as he would have—PO1 Neil Roberts, SrA Jason Cunningham, CPL Matthew Commons, SGT Bradley Crose, SPC Marc Anderson, and SGT Philip Svitak. Thank you for *your* sacrifices and God bless your families.

Thursday was John's induction into the Pentagon's Hall of Heroes. Large, beautiful storyboards with photos depicting John's life hung just outside the hall and we congregated there until it was time to be seated. After a few speeches, the most amazing of which came from then-Secretary of the Air Force Heather Wilson, Mom and I were escorted to the stage. Mom spoke for a minute before tears took her voice, and I stepped to the podium. I *needed* to talk about my brother, to share a sister's thoughts. And then, watching John be inducted to the Hall of Fame, made my heart swell with the pride I've always had in him. Again, he would be so humbled.

Finally, Friday's ceremony was the unveiling of John's name on the Air Force Memorial. Seven hundred people were expected to attend but 1,200 showed up. On the way to the memorial, our vans passed countless people hurrying to get there, and one of them made me cry. It was an Air Force officer in a flight suit; he stopped to salute us as we raced past. I cried because I understood the significance of that salute: An officer doesn't initiate a salute to an enlisted man. He did it as a sign of respect to John and to us. Thank you, kind officer. We saw you.

After John's name was revealed on the memorial, TSgt John A. Chapman—Afghanistan, Windsor Locks, CT, then-Chief Master Sergeant of the Air Force Kaleth Wright posthumously promoted him from Technical Sergeant to Master Sergeant. I knew it was coming, but it was still special because John had wanted to reach that rank before retirement. It came a little late, but he deserved it.

At the end of the ceremony, hundreds of those in attendance—military and civilian men and women—were led in memorial pushups, including me. It was, and will probably forever be, the largest group of memorial pushups held at the Air Force Memorial. I had participated in all memorial pushups up to that point, and I wasn't going to miss this one. It was literally planking room only.

During the run-up to the Medal of Honor ceremony in 2018, I received countless messages from strangers, thanking our family for John's patriotism, bravery, and sacrifice. Many of them related ways they chose to honor him. Mike Lincoln, brewer and owner of Noble Jay Brewing Company in Niantic, Connecticut, developed a beer called Chappy's Red Lager. He said it was one of his best sellers. Unfortunately, the 2020 "year of fear" kept him from remaining open and destroyed his dream. Thank you, Mike, for honoring John, our military, veterans, and first responders. I pray you find a new dream or resurrect your first one. You are a wonderful human being.

When I returned home after the Medal of Honor celebration week, I received a message from someone who touched me deeply.

> Hello Lori, my name is Tammy Ryan. I am trying to find a relative of Sgt John Chapman. I was wondering if you are his sister. I read the many reports of what this brave airman did and was

in awe. If you are his sister, I simply had to tell someone how proud, how truly proud, I am to know this man loved his country and his fellow military operators so much that he laid down his life to save them. His story is that of a true hero. What he did is nothing short of heroic, and admiration doesn't begin to explain it. I thought about what I could do to honor him . . . something special. I love dogs. I've always had one or two. I am getting a new Doberman puppy, and his name will be Chapman, and we will call him Chappy. He will be a symbol of the honor, sacrifice, and bravery of an American hero. Every time we say his name, we will remember. Every time someone asks me, "Why Chapman?" (which they will) I will tell them the story of a man, an airman, a husband, brother, and son who made the ultimate sacrifice. I will tell them how he fought like a warrior. I hope you know that you and your family will always be in my prayers, and that this is one American that is forever grateful. And to Sgt John Chapman, Godspeed, rest well good and faithful servant. You have all I can give, my gratitude, my respect, my utmost pride. My bold, brave Doberman will have an honorable name.

When I messaged Tammy again, she said she had gotten an Old English Bulldog instead of a Doberman. Her handsome boy's registered name is Sergeant Chapman, and he is now seventy-five pounds of pure muscle. He is a reminder that heroes exist, and we're so fortunate to have them. She has a video in which the breeder says, "Look at him. He's not afraid of anything." Tammy remembers thinking, "He's the perfect dog to carry the name Chapman.

In the time since getting Chapman, Tammy's goal has been reached time and again. "People do ask about his name. The story of your brother has been spread countless times because this dog bears that name. A few have talked to me later and said they looked up his story. It's an amazing story that we all talk about. The story of John now gets told by other people. That was my plan: The dog is the message." Thank you, Tammy, for one of the coolest ways to honor John, for sharing his story with anyone who cares to ask, and for your own patriotism.

Two months after the Medal of Honor ceremonies, in October 2018, John's upgraded military award was reflected on the Special Tactics Memorial at Hurlburt Field, Fort Walton Beach, Florida. That was the same weekend the 24th SOW building was dedicated to him and the first time Hurlburt runways were closed for an air show to honor a fallen hero. Mike West drove General Goldfein in his Cobra down the middle of the runway—something that may never be done again. During that weekend, John also had one of the presidential fleet of airplanes named for him, so depending on the passenger, "his" plane would be Air Force Two. I think that is pretty damn cool … first a ship, then a vice-presidential aircraft!

I've already mentioned *Alone at Dawn*. It was written to introduce Combat Control and to reveal the truth of John's actions—what really happened on Takur Ghar—and the after-action lies and cover-up. It was personal for me. I wanted John's last day to finally be portrayed honestly, supported by facts and video, so everyone would know he *earned* that Medal of Honor (actually, two); and that the grossly watered-down citation isn't a fraction of the real story. John is no longer here to set the record straight, so Dan Schilling and I did. *Alone at Dawn* honors not only John but the tenacity and integrity of all Combat Controllers. I, again, thank Dan for ferreting out the truth among the lies. His access to people and information that I would have never had was paramount to bypassing the disinformation and getting to reality. Our book, a New York Times best-seller, was released in June 2019 and is the subject of an upcoming movie being produced by Thruline Entertainment and MGM. Stay tuned!

On March 4, 2020, the eighteenth anniversary of John's death, Medina Annex, located on Lackland AFB and the beginning of the Special Tactics training pipeline, was renamed Chapman Annex. Now, when young trainees enter, the first name they'll see is Chapman after a brave Air Force warrior and someone they may strive to emulate.

While at Lackland, we were able to visit the Chapman Training Complex to see what life as a trainee looks like. Lt Col Eric Bein, then the 326th Training Squadron commander, gave us a tour of the complex, including their Medal of Honor display in a main hallway, and Chapman Classroom, which had been renovated by trainees a year earlier. One wall starts with photo collages of John from childhood to Combat Control and then transitions to the battle on Takur Ghar. On the far right is a celebration of

John's Medal of Honor that was hand-painted by three talented trainees: M. Alvarez-Santiago, C. Armstrong, and C. Winn. On the opposite side of the room, the wall is covered with four giant photos of John with the American flag painted as the backdrop. The wall ends with his Medal of Honor citation. The young men and women took their self-appointed task to heart in making the classroom worthy of bearing John's name, and the result is so much more impressive than I can state here. Hooyah, Bulldogs!!

Before leaving the base, Mom and I were invited to attend a graduation of trainees who had made it through Basic Training and earned the rank of Airman Basic. Way back in the "old days," either the Air Force didn't make a big deal of graduation day, or John didn't. Either way, none of us went to his graduation, so we were thrilled to have the opportunity to join proud families who traveled untold distances to watch their trainees become airmen. At the end of their graduation, all newly-minted airmen have to stay in formation until they are "tapped out" by a family member. Unfortunately, some have families who cannot attend, so Mom and I found one such young man and released him. That made me happy.

Congratulations to all who become airmen and thank you for your service, but special congrats to those who graduated on March 6, 2020. It was an honor to watch you officially become airmen. Godspeed in all you do.

You're going to love this story, my friends! Since 2000, the Air Force Academy classes have chosen exemplars during freshman year; someone they wish to emulate throughout the rest of their time at the academy. One of the requirements was to choose an officer since they'll all be officers upon graduation. The Class of 2026 originally suggested over 50 people. After months of research, the Exemplar Committee narrowed it down to 14 nominees, all of whom were excellent choices, but one was enlisted. The academy leadership ... or I should say, those in charge of overseeing the exemplar choices ... shut down John's nomination because he wasn't an officer. Previous other classes had also nominated him, but none were as determined as the class of 2026. Under the leadership of Class President, then-Cadet 3rd Class (C3C) Kobe Achu, the committee fought long and hard to overcome the rule they felt was unfair. It was a virtual hill many were willing to "die" on.

Then-C3C Nicholas Gierach was one of many who had nominated John, and he was as tenacious as anyone. He, along with Kobe, then-C3C Lauren Mirande (Exemplar Chairperson), C3C Jack Pleus (Exemplar Assistant Chairperson), and the rest of the committee, argued that John *was* a great example of leadership, even though he was not the designated leader. He exemplified everything any other exemplar had, and they were not inclined to accept defeat.

The young men and women of the committee leapfrogged over each level of bureaucracy, steadfast in their belief that John was just as qualified to be their exemplar as anyone else. After months of hard-fought advances, they were finally granted the right to include him as one of the 14 nominees. As classmates gathered in a large auditorium to hear who won the popular vote, no one could have anticipated the result. When John's name was announced, the class erupted in thunderous cheers. The class had voted for him in a landslide victory—over 80%!

In September 2023, family and friends gathered in Mitchell Hall for dinner and the official public announcement that MSgt John "Sarge" Chapman would be the Class of 2026 Exemplar. They assigned him the new moniker in deference to his rank, and they enthusiastically yelled it anytime "Class of 2026" was mentioned. What a fun night! We met so many amazing young men and women. Nick Gierach shared with me a routine he developed during the fight to include John. After hours, the Medal of Honor Hall offered the solitude he needed to keep going. He spoke internally to many of the heroes there, asking them to help. When Nick came to John's picture, he would stop and tell John, "We're not giving up." After a quick prayer, and feeling bolstered, Nick was ready to take the next day with positivity and courage. I was reminded of John's letters to me while he fought through the pipeline: *I'm struggling, but I'm not giving up.*

What an impressive group of young people; those who will be leaders in our military in years to come. I pray for their continued pursuit of what is right and for their safety in all they endeavor.

If you want to witness the reveal, meet some of the committee members, and get goosebumps when you hear the cheers, look up "USAFA Class of 2026 Exemplar Reveal" on YouTube. I cried the first time I saw it … and a few times after that, too. Sarge!

★ ★ ★ ★

You cannot get more American than cadets at our Air Force Academy, but it seems the desire to honor John is not exclusive to Americans. Before I wrap up this chapter, I must share the story of a kindhearted Scotsman.

About ten years ago, Kenny was on a business trip to Jackson, Wyoming, and stayed in a small cabin of the Cowboy Village. One morning, he heard someone playing the fiddle and stepped outside to investigate. He did not talk with the gentleman but enjoyed the sweet sound coming from the neighbor as he prepared to smoke a brisket all day for dinner with colleagues. Later, with evening approaching and Kenny finishing dinner preparations, the gentleman emerged from his cabin, following his nose to the source of the glorious smell. He introduced himself and Kenny knew immediately the man was "not from these parts."

Robert Sheerins was surprised when Kenny asked what part of Scotland he called home. And the friendship began. They only talked for about an hour or so because the colleagues arrived for dinner, but Kenny made two plates of brisket with all the fixings for Robert and his wife. That was the last time they saw each other in person. Robert departed before Kenny returned the next day but left a note of thanks that included his contact information. The two have kept in contact ever since. At some point, Kenny told Robert about John and *Alone at Dawn*. He said, "I think Robert ordered the book while we were talking." After reading it, Robert told him that he paints portraits, and he was so moved by John's story

285

that he wanted to do one of John for me. Kenny first thought they would surprise me, but quickly decided I needed to choose the photo. When he told me what Robert wanted to do, I was amazed and excited.

I chose the last photo taken of John and me, but later found out it was supposed to be just John. When I offered to pick a different one, Robert said he wouldn't have it. He shared his progress with Kenny, who teased me about knowing something I didn't.

Our original plan was to visit Robert and his wife in Scotland to receive the painting, but he did not want to wait. Robert put it in the mail and when I opened it, I could not contain my emotions. The photo I chose was taken in my grandmother's living room, but Robert wanted a different background. He put so much heart and thought into it, deciding on a sunset because, as he said, "The setting sun and the warmth of the colours seemed in many ways appropriate to you seeing your brother under the circumstances."

We are still going to visit Robert and his family in Scotland, and I cannot wait to thank him properly. It will never cease to amaze me how many people continue to honor John in so many unique, thoughtful, and personal ways, especially those who never met any of us. Thank you so much, Robert, for blessing me with your beautiful tribute to John.

John never played the fiddle, but he loved music, so I think it's appropriate to end this chapter with two songs. One honors the pain people endure and how they overcome, and the other honors not only John but all in Special Tactics. They were written by Windsor Locks alum, friend, and classmate of John's, Dan Castonguay. His professional name is Dan Tracey and he is the cofounder, lead singer, and lead guitarist of the band, Save the World. The very first song he wrote for the band was "Bleed." It is included on their first album titled One and was inspired by John, though not about him.

According to the band's Facebook page, "Bleed" is both cathartic and catchy, a gut-punch melody that unpacks the tattoo trend in a profound way. "The meaning of the song hit me when I was getting ready for that morning's sessions—the pain of getting tattoos allows people to let out their pain and their dreams. It's a release."[8]

The first song released from their second album, Two, is "Defenders of the Faith," which is a warning to our enemies that we have the best of the best to defend us. The accompanying videos bring both songs to life in ways that are sure to give you chills. Look them up, watch, and listen. Thank you, Dan, for your undying support of our military men and women, and thank you for remembering a neighborhood kid who did something great.

---

[8] Dan Tracey, "About the Band," About the World, 2016, www.facebook.com/savetheworldband/.

21

A Sister's Thoughts

*It's hard to turn the page when you know someone won't
be in the next chapter, but the story must go on.*
~ Thomas Wilder

John never tried to be perfect, but he did aspire to be
the best John Chapman he could ever be. He stumbled
along the way and made some poor decisions, but I
think he lived with confidence, compassion, humor,
intellect, loyalty, integrity, and so much more. His goal
wasn't to live a flawless life; what fun would that be?
Whether consciously or not, John tried to leave people
better than he found them, or at least no worse off, and
he did it throughout his lifetime. We could all learn
something from that. Though his life ended much too
soon, he lived it to the fullest, sometimes on the edge,
and he accomplished everything he'd dreamed about as
a small child. He traveled the world, cultivated countless
friendships, made his family proud, fell in love and
became a daddy, and left a legacy everywhere he went. He
became the hero that his adolescent self had envisioned.
We lost him long before any of us expected, and I miss

him every day, but the life he lived was fuller than most who reach twice his age. What more can anyone ask?

So, nature or nurture? I still think it's both, but the scale favors the nature argument. After learning about John from his youngest days, how can any other conclusion be drawn? The nurturing from family and friends absolutely factored in, there's no doubt, but it could not have changed who he naturally was, could it? Maybe it could. Maybe our simple, busy, and easy-going upbringing enhanced what God put inside him.

What I *do* know is that I am the luckiest and most blessed sister in the world, and I'm not afraid to brag about it. I offer no apologies. I grew up with three fantastic siblings who are so much a part of me; Kevin, John, and Tammy helped mold who I am today. Back then, I could never have imagined living a day without any of them. Now, I face the daily pain of having lost one brother. When he died, each of us died a little too. Mom has never been the same. How could she be? Maybe none of us are. Dad was crushed in ways he never shared, but two years later, he joined John after suffering a heart attack.

We all face this kind of deep, gut-wrenching pain in different ways. Some keep it private. Some feel the need to get on with life and not dwell on it. Some cannot seem to find their way again. How one handles his or her pain is as varied as there are people. I usually find comfort in talking about John, hearing stories about him, listening to his voice in videos, looking at photos of him, celebrating him, and wanting to be around others who love him as much as I do.

There are days that find me joyful in the memories of my younger brother, and there are just as many days in which I cry as if it's the first time I'm hearing that he's gone. My body is wracked with physical pain over not having John in my life and over knowing the facts about what he had to endure in his last hour. I can place myself alongside him, feeling how desperate he must have been when he realized he had been left behind. I know he didn't have time for self-pity, but if he felt abandonment, even for an instant, what did that do to him? I think the reality is closer to the philosophy he imparted on Summa Stelly: "When you're deep in the shit, you don't think about anything but the men you're with and getting out of the situation one way or another." I *pray* he didn't have time for nagging thoughts in his last hour.

For a time after John was killed, I hated God. How could He let this happen to my brother—to all of us? When Mom had the priest whispering comforting words in her living room, I stayed in the kitchen. I didn't want to hear those cliché phrases: "God has a plan." "Everything happens for a reason." I was so angry and wanted nothing to do with the God we had been brought up to know and love. At some point, I don't know when, perhaps a few years, I realized that, ultimately, John had acted of his own free will. *He* decided to go with that team even though he didn't have to go. *He* decided to join them in their attempt at a second infiltration to find the downed teammate. *He* chose to take the lead when his leader fell short. *He* chose to attack their attackers and to press on toward others. And in the end, *he* chose to rise from shelter, from possible salvation, to lay down suppressive fire to protect the eighteen men of the incoming Quick Reaction Force. God gave us free will, and John never shied away from using his. Once I realized God *wasn't* to blame, I made peace with John's decisions and with God. But I still miss him every single day, and the pain never goes away. It might ease a bit, but there are always times when one random memory or song or smell or event brings it back in full force.

I am now working on forgiveness. Lewis B. Smedes said, "To forgive is to set a prisoner free and discover that the prisoner was you." My desire to shed a glaring light on those who lied to keep their brand clean and those who mistreated our family was suffocating. I wanted everyone to know their deeds—to lay it out there for all to see, but then felt guilty for having those thoughts. I could feel something tugging at me, dragging me toward forgiveness, but I wasn't ready. I had a scathing open letter written and ready for publication when I shared its concept with my niece Sierra. She was eighteen years old and so much wiser than I. She reflected for just a moment and quietly said, "But how would you really feel if you made it public?" It was a simple question that made me think deeply, and it was another nudge toward forgiveness. I'm embarrassed to admit it, but about a year after my talk with Sierra, apparently having moved away from grace again, I tried to get the letter published and felt relief when no one would accept it. So, while I have not reached forgiveness, I am working toward it. I may not ever get there. It's a constant struggle, and I still find myself getting sucked back into wanting retribution. What I find most difficult is being reminded that hubris resulted in my brother's death, and those guilty of it have gotten to go on living and loving their families … and lying about their "virtues." John is gone. It's permanent, just like my grief, and I don't know what forgiveness looks like. I need to remember that those who disrespected John and our family will have to answer for it when they pass from this earth. I am human, and I am trying. Another quote, this one of unknown origin, is what I am struggling to get: "Forgive others, not because they deserve forgiveness, but because you deserve peace." Amen to that.

Focusing on our childhood, I wouldn't trade growing up with my family for the world. Yes, the six of us were crammed into a small, three-bedroom, one-bathroom house, but that didn't seem to matter. (Ok, I *would* have appreciated another bathroom.) Those five people were my world. Mom and Dad provided for and guided each of us individually and together. They instilled work ethic, compassion, and so many other good things. They supported each of us as we twirled a baton, swung a bat, learned to swim, or played a geeky accordion. They taught us we could do anything we put our minds to doing. We had shoulders to cry on when we were devastated by the angst of youth and got pats on the back when we did something exceptional. Mom and Dad weren't perfect, but they were perfect for *us*.

Then there are Kevin, John, and Tammy. We had our moments, for sure; some I remember, but most have been lost to the insignificance of youthful strife. Whether my memories have faded or changed or grown over the past decades, they're mine to treasure and share. When I was a petulant tween, I occasionally wished aloud that I had been an only child. Thank God that He knew better. The four of us grew up with sibling secrets, outrageous fun, epic fights, and ultimate solidarity. We were truly "all for one and one for all," and I am so proud of the man John became and the people Kevin and Tammy continue to be.

As we grew and forged our own ways in the world, there were times when it felt we weren't as close as we once were, but the reality was our closeness had merely changed. It was mature. We all brought something to the table and, usually, John's contribution was laughter. He was so good at making us laugh—at him, at ourselves, at anything. Dan Castonguay echoed that sentiment. "Your brother was a funny SOB. Ya either wanted to slap him or laugh at yourself with him. How did he do that?"

When Kevin, John, and I visited Dad after he moved to Michigan, we were in our early twenties but acted like we were ten years younger. Dad took us to his favorite pizza joint for dinner. We realized there was only one slice left on the pedestal, and Dad sat back to observe. The three of us looked straight ahead, each with a different view of the prize, our eyes darting from the pizza to our competitors and back to the pizza. John broke the standoff by grabbing the slice, licking it, and placing it back onto the pedestal. He crossed his arms, elbows on the edge of the table, and asked with feigned manners,

"Anyone want the last slice?" Dad almost fell out of his chair he laughed so hard. Kevin and I conceded defeat and watched John eat as slowly as he could, savoring his victory.

And that's how it was. John could take even the most ordinary circumstance and turn it into something more. And why not? We could all probably benefit from such lightness. I miss those times. Don't get me wrong, I still laugh hard, but those times with John will always be such special memories.

While Kevin was embarking on a career in computers (don't ask me exactly what he did, I just know he was really good at it), Tammy was entering college, and I was on my own and working, John joined the Air Force. It would never have crossed my mind that he'd go that route, but once he made the decision, I knew it was the right one for him. Windsor Locks was a wonderful place to be raised, but it couldn't give him what he craved. He had talked about traveling the world; he always wanted to push himself for bigger and better things, to test the fiber of his being. The Air Force was his ticket to achieving those lifelong dreams, and he went for it. He accomplished far beyond the bounds of anything he could have dreamed as a child.

This is the chapter for me to express my thoughts, and I need to include one that has been on my mind since we received that dreaded call in March 2002. I'm headed in a different direction right now—one that may be a little uncomfortable for some. Honestly, it is a subject that countless others have asked me to explain. One was actually very angry as he questioned me, "Why isn't John in Arlington [National Cemetery]? He *earned* that honor."

Yes, he did. John gave his all to any job he did from auto mechanic to Combat Controller. He embodied the saying, "If you're going to do a job, do it right the first time." John's loyalty to the team and his need to do the very best for them earned him the Medal of Honor and the coveted right to be buried in Arlington National Cemetery. I know that any of our military and their spouses can be buried there, but John went over and above with his service to our country, to his team, to the QRF, and to us. Like my impassioned friend said, John *earned* the right to be buried in Arlington, near his fallen comrades, some of whom died the same day. But he's not there and that makes me quite sad, even angry at times, if I can be frank. I know men who go to Arlington specifically to visit the headstones of fallen brothers. Those heroes are never alone; always remembered and sought out, even by strangers.

I have *no* doubt people will look for John merely because he is one of the newest Medal of Honor recipients and the first to have video proof of his actions. He is also the first Air Force Airman to receive it since Vietnam. They will be surprised to find that he is not in the resting place of heroes and not many will make the trek to western Pennsylvania. Once Val's dad Jim Novak can no longer visit his gravesite, no one other than family and close friends will care that he's there. Jim promised my dad that he would always take care of John's grave since he lives five walking minutes away, but there will come a time when he cannot do it. What then?

To be crystal clear, this is not an indictment of Valerie's decision to bury John in Pennsylvania. She was operating on shock, lack of sleep, and grief as decisions had to be made quickly, and she thought they would move back to Pennsylvania to be near her parents. My brain understands that, but it doesn't make the result any easier for my heart to accept. Understanding cannot change what I wish deep within—that John rests where he paid with his life to be: Arlington National Cemetery, alongside thousands of other American heroes and visited by millions.

After learning so much of what John had to endure to become a Combat Controller; after finding the truth of his heroic actions on that desolate mountaintop in Afghanistan; after meeting the men who were his military family, men cut from the same cloth as he; after reading book after book about brave men from World War II, Vietnam, Operation Just Cause, and other wars—I miss something that I never even experienced: serving in our military. Though I would never have done the badass things of these heroes, it's the camaraderie, the brotherhood, and the lifelong bonds that I miss even though they were never mine to lose. I've witnessed time and again as my husband has met teammates from long ago in some of the most random places, and they pick up right where they left off. It would have been the same way for John had he lived.

Ultimately, I am thankful that John made the choices he did—for himself, for his family, for his brothers, and for this country. He took it on for all of us, forging ahead at his own pace, and showing the world what true heroism looks like. But he didn't just affect people at the end of his life; he changed lives throughout his almost thirty-seven years. Now, when you see his name in history books or on some website, you will know how he came to be the man who laid down his life for us all.

Don't stop when you're tired, stop when you are done.
~ Marilyn Monroe

As our literary bonfire has been reduced to glowing embers and the cocoa has lost its warmth, my heart is filled with gratitude over sharing John's life with you, my dear friends. I pray that something he did or said resonates with you, encourages you, brings back a long-forgotten memory, and entertains you immensely. God bless you always and safe travels wherever you may go.

Acknowledgments

Among the things you can give and still keep are your word, a smile, and a grateful heart.
~ Zig Ziglar

Without the memories of my family, John's childhood friends, and his military buddies, this story could never be told. They were willing to go back in time, crawl through the mental cobwebs, and share some of their most special memories of John.

First, I could never have completed this book without the continued (mostly) gentle nudges from my husband Kenny. He knew I could do this even when doubt paralyzed me. This smart man had great intuition about when and how much to push. Thank you, Kenny, for your patience and encouragement. I love you.

I appreciate my family—Terry Chapman, Kevin Chapman, Tammy and David Klein, Tess Chapman, and Valerie Nessel—for setting aside any reservations they may have had and for their eagerness to tell their stories. I also am thankful that my father Gene Chapman thought to send a letter to John's squadron. John's story could have been told without Dad's correspondence but having it available revealed some of the thought processes during important turning points in his life.

To John's childhood friends, I am indebted to you. Thank you, Skeet Tersavich, our loving brother from another mother; Tom Allen, our diving coach who also became family; John's best friends—Brian Topor, David Wrabel, Mike DuPont, and Mike Toce. He loved you 'til the end.

Thanks to those friends who were in John's life for a shorter time, but whom he cared for dearly—Bill Brooks, Jimmy Grandhal, Lynn Noyes Klein, Suzy Lindberg Brinegar, Kelly Cray Savery, Chris Daniel, Dan Tracey Castonguay, Danny Walsh, Rob LeBreche, and Anthony Burke. You all meant more to John than you know. Much gratitude also goes to Tammy Ryan—though a stranger to John and our family, you still found a way to reach out and share your loving story.

To all of John's military buddies, it was difficult to decide which stories to share because you stepped up and offered so many! As with John's childhood friends, some of you only knew John a short time and some were friends for years. God bless you all for sitting down with me or for writing letters. I cannot express enough how much it means to me. You're all badasses! Thank you to Mike West, Ron Childress, Jeremy Shoop, Summa Stelly, Ken Rodriguez, Billy Sasser, Pat Elko, Mike Lamonica, Bruce Dixon, David Gendron, Steve Coronato, Travis Woodworth, Kurt Buller, James Taylor, Kyle Stanbro, Bart Decker, and again, Kenny Longfritz (as John's First Sergeant).

Ultimately, thanks to all who trusted me to tell their stories so the world may know John as we did. If, by some cruel chance, I have forgotten someone, please know I am eternally grateful for your help in sharing John's epic life of mischief, failures, compassion, perseverance, and triumph.

I need to thank my sister-in-law Connie and brother Kevin again because they furnished the final piece—a publisher. Through an event at church, Connie met a woman whose husband is a publisher in Colorado Springs. She excitedly shared the information with Kevin who passed it along to me. He began by asking how the book was coming along, and I gave my usual sad response, "Well, it's been done for quite some time, but I need help making it better. Still don't have a publisher." That's when he told me about Dave Sheets and Believers Book Services. Thanks to Kevin for also not giving up on me when I thought my "end of the road" had turned into a cliff into the abyss.

Thank you, Dave Sheets, for wanting to help me tell the story of John's life through Believers Book Services. You and your staff made me start believing in myself again. It was a difficult process at times, but the encouragement you all offered enabled me to push forward. Roberta was assigned to keep me on task and I did not make it easy for her. Special thanks to her for the patience and grace she gave me. May God continue to bless all from Believers Book Services with the ability to help those of us who need it. I offer much appreciation to Roberta Nichols, Marcus Costantino, Josh Vogt, Cristina Wright, Amy Sinnott, Terry Dugan, eBookBurner Technologies, and Justin Shreeves. You are special people.

Thank you again to my readers. I pray something in John's life has inspired you to be more, to do more, to see the invisible people all around you, and to offer what you can. And to live your life to the fullest without hesitation.

Lastly, I thank God for blessing me with family, friends, amazing partners, and the ability to express myself on paper. I have always loved to write and have had brief moments of greatness . . . in my mind anyway. I recognize that I cannot accomplish my dreams without the help of others, nor without Him. I also thank God for choosing me to grow up in the Chapman family alongside three amazing siblings. I am indeed blessed.

About the Author

Writing, to me, is simply thinking through my fingers.
~ Isaac Asimov

Lori Chapman Longfritz grew up in blue-collar New England in a time when people knew their neighbors and embraced the closeness that community offered. Though she misses living on the East Coast, especially the fresh seafood and the breathtaking autumn colors, Lori now enjoys her life in the "forever west" town of Cheyenne, Wyoming, home of the Frontier Days "Daddy of Them All" rodeo. She lives with her husband Kenny, their son John, and furry girl Maya. Much to Lori's delight, her daughter Rachel lives across town with her husband Kaleb and kids Stetson and Paislee. Life is good.

Lori is co-author of the New York Times Best Seller, *Alone at Dawn*—the prime source about John's Air Force career in Combat Control and the actions that eventually earned him the Medal of Honor. She knew his story had to be told, and occasionally speaks about it, but has always wanted to share who John was at his core. That dream has finally come true.

Lori is also a board member of the First There Foundation, an organization formed in October 2021 by former CCT Eric Lionheart to help support members of the Air Force Combat Control community and their families. She has benefitted from their mental health retreats and, in the process, has been able to begin healing from losing John over twenty years ago. The long-term goal of First There is to be able to help anyone, military or civilian, in dealing with mental health issues. This organization is dear to Lori's heart, and John would have been an enthusiastic supporter. Please visit their website for more information at https://www.1stthere.org/.

Besides writing, Lori loves to sew—from Halloween costumes to Christmas stockings, curtains, and even a Buffalo Bills blazer for Kenny, a diehard Bills fan. Go Bills! She is trying to turn her brown thumb into, at the very least, a light green thumb, and is interested in learning about beekeeping and ham radio. Lori and Kenny love entertaining because visiting with family and friends is the best therapy anyone could want. You can never go wrong with barbeques and game nights!